# Bath Bombs

# Bath Bombs

ELAINE STAVERT

GUILD OF MASTER
CRAFTSMAN PUBLICATIONS

First published 2008 by
**Guild of Master Craftsman Publications Ltd**
Castle Place, 166 High Street,
Lewes, East Sussex BN7 1XU

Text © Elaine Stavert, 2008
© in the Work GMC Publications, 2008

ISBN: 978-1-86108-615-0

**Associate Publisher:** Jonathan Bailey
**Production Manager:** Jim Bulley
**Managing Editor:** Gerrie Purcell
**Project Editor:** Virginia Brehaut
**Managing Art Editor:** Gilda Pacitti
**Designer:** Jo Patterson
**Picture Researcher:** Hedda Roennevig

Set in Gill Sans and Ribbon

Colour origination by **GMC Reprographics**
Printed and bound in Thailand by Kyodo Nation Printing

# Why we love bath bombs

Fizzing and spinning and releasing a scent
Relaxing and soaking, hours in the bath were spent
Softening the skin and easing our pains
Warming and comforting when pouring with rain

Hangovers, jet lag and exams were a breeze
After sports, exercise or yoga on knees
Calming and soothing for children and grannies
Potions for the heart if you want to get married

All of these things we love and adore
About our great bath bombs... we just want to make more!

# Contents

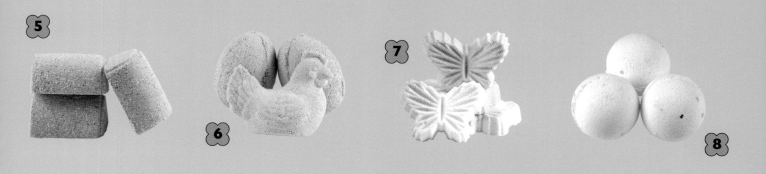

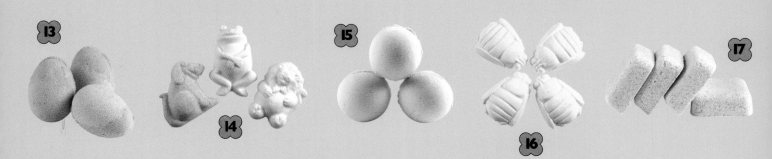

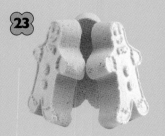

# Introduction

When I was first asked to write this book a few people said to me 'can you really have a whole book on bath bombs'? The answer, as you will see when you read on, is 'yes, absolutely', for although bath bombs may be a contemporary innovation, they are just another step in the history of bathing, with aromatic oils, perfumes and herbs having been used since time immemorial to anoint, scent and cleanse the body for the purpose of worship, hygiene, medical and spiritual wellbeing.

## So what exactly is a bath bomb?

A bath bomb is made with just three main ingredients, citric acid, bicarbonate of soda and water, mixed together, moulded and left to dry hard. The resulting 'bomb' is then popped into a warm bath, fizzing and effervescing as it is immersed in the water, releasing any aromatic oils, herbs and butters you may also have added to your mixture, leaving the water fragrantly scented, soft and moisturizing.

Bicarbonate of soda, $NaHCO_3$, also known as baking soda (not to be confused with baking powder, which is a mixture of cream of tartar and bicarbonate of soda), is a white powdery substance made up of three elements, carbon (C), hydrogen (H) and sodium (Na). The Na comes from natron, which was mined by the ancient Egyptians from the dry beds of lakes, and from the banks of the River Nile. It was used for washing and embalming mummies, helping them to smell fresh for longer. Other uses by the Egyptians were for exfoliating the body and cleaning the teeth, as a deodorant, cleaning cuts and making glass. Bicarbonate of soda has numerous other applications and is widely used today as natural cleaning ingredient, neutralizer and in cooking.

The other ingredient required to make a bath bomb is citric acid. Citric acid, $C_6H_8O_7$, is an organic acid existing in many fruits and vegetables, but mainly citrus fruits, with lime and lemon containing particularly high concentrations. It is a naturally occurring white crystalline acid and is used as a flavouring, food additive and preservative in fizzy drinks and beer, as a detergent and cleaner, and in cosmetics and pharmaceuticals. Citric acid is naturally present in almost all forms of life and is widely refined today by fermenting molasses, cane sugar and dextrose.

Now that you have drawn your warm bath, tossed in your bath bomb and are soaking in your tub with aromatic oils wafting around the room, close your eyes, let your mind drift back in time and read on to the following pages to find out how our ancestors may have bathed in similar ways.

# History of bathing

Many ancient cultures were united in believing that the spiritual energy of water was one of the divine forces of nature and as a source of energy would heal, cleanse and purify the spirit; it was therefore often used in religious ceremonies and for marking the rites of passage.

No life form can survive without water. Our bodies are in fact 70% H$_2$O and many cultures' beliefs feature water being present at the moment of creation. Bathing gives us a feeling of comfort and security, peace and contentment, perhaps subconsciously reminding us of the protective time in our mother's womb.

It is hard to tell who were the first ancient civilizations to bathe, but there are certain periods in history when dirt and cleanliness have come in and out of fashion throughout the world. Bathing has meant very different things to many cultures over the centuries, with some completely scouring and cleansing their bodies and others declining to dip their big toe into water.

*Throughout history and spanning all cultures, bathing habits and rituals are incredibly diverse and always changing.*

# Egyptian

As Egypt emerged as the central area of the western Eurasian cosmetic trade, hot water bathing and perfume were highly important. Records show that they were prolific bathers, spending hours on their ablutions, after which they smothered their bodies with perfumed oils to nourish their skin.

These blends of precious oils were often made by priests who were used to creating perfumes for worship and rituals. History shows that the ancient Egyptians bathed at home in a separate, designated bathing room in the house using a perfumed cream made from lime and oil.

# Greeks

Ancient Greeks washed before praying, before embarking on a journey and as a guest on arrival at a wealthy man's house. During feasts and banquets they were offered a bath followed by the anointment of expensive, aromatic oils. The Greeks also bathed for health reasons, often having a washstand at home called a 'labrum' and a bath that was set in the ground.

Bathing for the Greeks was a social occasion with individual hip baths situated around the main pool where the men would chat, play dice and perhaps have a drink and a snack. There were also rooms for cold and warm baths, which were similar, but less sophisticated than the later Roman baths. The poor would have to use the local well!

Baths were also available in Greek gymnasiums, which were reserved only for the middle–upper class and the wealthy to develop and maintain their strength on the outdoor exercise fields. Discussions and lectures were also held at Athenian academies and lyceums where Plato and Aristotle founded their schools of philosophy in the fourth century.

At the gymnasiums men oiled and dusted their naked bodies before exercising, playing ball games or wrestling, after which they scraped down their sweaty, oily skin with a metal instrument called a 'strigil'. They would then wash off the excess with unheated water from a bath or basin. It was considered much more butch to bathe in unheated water, and the recorded debates of effeminate warm-water bathing versus manly cold-water bathing were later embraced by Victorian men studying the classical Greek scriptures.

*An ancient Greek gymnasium, the figure on the left holds a 'strigil' used for scraping oil and sweat from the skin.*

*The magnificent Roman Baths in the City of Bath, England.*

# Romans

Roman baths emanated first from the Italian peninsula out into the Roman Empire in the second century AD. By that time the splashing, soaking, steaming and oiling of their bodies was part of everyday life.

Life in the Roman era was short, with many not achieving an age of more than 30 years, medicinal bathing was therefore considered to be of great importance, with the belief that it was preventative for a vast range of illnesses from liver, intestine, bowel and urinary complaints, to soothing boils, pustules and fevers. This encouraged the Romans to incorporate bathing as a part of their daily routine, mainly at the end of the working day where medicinal masseurs were also on hand at the communal baths.

Although most wealthy Romans built their own private baths in their villas, they also used the public baths and spas for socializing, where Romans from all classes and walks of life would also spend much of their leisure time. These social arenas, or clubs, contained libraries, meeting and lecture rooms, gymnasiums and gardens, the baths often being surrounded by shops, beauty salons, hairdressers, herbalists and brothels, with food and drink also available to purchase.

One of the oldest Roman baths still nearly intact is the Stabian Baths at Pompeii, circa 140 BC, where, similar to the Greeks, there was wrestling and play, followed by time in a warm room where their oiled bodies were scraped down, followed by a plunge pool or basin to wash with. Finally, there was a room with a cold plunge pool, followed by more oiling, scraping and massage with aromatic oils. Soap was not used at this point for bathing, only a rough version for laundry; soap factories have also been found in the remains of Pompeii for this reason.

The use of the Roman baths slowly died out with the decline of the Roman Empire, as the aqueducts supplying the water for the baths were destroyed, and the invading tribes were uninterested in the Roman way of bathing, so that by the eighth and ninth centuries the Roman baths were abandoned.

# Turkish baths

Tukish baths or 'hamam' were traditionally sited at mineral springs and were beautifully constructed from marble. The concept of the bath was brought over by the Muslims along with their bathing rituals, and mixed with the designs of the Roman bath. A typical Turkish bath consists of three rooms, one with a steaming hot bath, a warm room for washing with soap and water, and a cool room for resting and relaxation.

The Turkish bath was enjoyed socially by the rich and the poor and particularly by women to celebrate rites of passage such as weddings and births, religious holidays, and to beautify themselves with the treatments that were on offer. It was also customary to bring refreshments to the baths to share during and after bathing, such as sweets, fruit and drinks.

In the mid-nineteenth century, a Victorian version of the Turkish bath was created which was more like a sauna and reminiscent of a Roman bath. The idea caught on and hundreds of Victorian Turkish baths opened all over Britain and in other parts of the British Empire.

*Turkish baths became very popular in Victorian times. This picture shows a cool room for relaxing and resting.*

# The Middle Ages

From the late Middle Ages, although a few hot public baths still existed, there was a long period up to the eighteenth century when people did not wash regularly and never bathed in a bath. Visiting non-Westerners found the lack of European hygiene quite shocking. During this period not only were there few facilities and little opportunity of immersing the body in water, except perhaps in smelly rivers, but also soap was either very rough and caustic and mainly used for laundry, or later on with the importation of olive oil from southern Europe, expensive and highly taxed.

During this period many people believed that it was enough for the linen of their clothes and bed sheets to absorb their dirt and perspiration, thereby keeping them clean enough with perfume and cologne masking their sweaty scent.

In 1791 a French chemist named Nicholas Leblanc patented a process for making sodium carbonate from salt; this is the ingredient that, combined with fat and oils, produces soap and enabled soap to be manufactured on a larger and cheaper scale.

# Japanese bathing

In Japanese culture, bathing has been a ritual for thousands of years, a cleansing of the body and the soul, a place for reflection and a time for family and community. Bathing is performed with families at home or with friends at communal baths with temple-like buildings called 'sentos', or at 'onsen' – hot springs. Baths are usually taken at the end of the day after an evening meal and before bedtime, or at a time for self-reflection.

The first bathing-related area that you would usually come to in a Japanese home is the 'datsuiba', a changing room usually screened off from the main bathing area by a sliding, frosted glass door. The bathroom itself is usually situated in the inner-most part of the house with a view of the Japanese garden, linking the bather with the natural world outside.

Japanese bathing begins by sitting on a small plastic or wooden stool which is situated next to a low set of taps on the wall. The bather then fills up a wooden bucket from the hot tub and pours it over the body several times to rinse the dirt from the skin. The bather then enters the hot bath, soaking the body and softening the skin until it is ready for scrubbing. Then, back on the stool, the bather lathers and scrubs the skin thoroughly, rinses again with the bucket and enters the tub for another soaking, the body is finally rinsed again with cold water. This process should not be rushed; time should be taken to contemplate, enjoy and socialize.

Nowadays there are less people using the 'sentos', as modern pipework has been introduced to the home, encouraging more home bathing and less community bathing. The Western bathing habits of showering have also found their way into the big cities and are popular with the younger generation.

*A Japanese bath with a fantastic view of the natural world outside.*

# Jewish bathing

A 'Mikvah' is a 3,000-year-old Jewish spiritual purification ritual, when only after fully cleaning and grooming every single part of the body the bather may immerse themself in pure, natural water of a divine source, with nothing coming between the water and the body, thus purifying and renewing the spirit. These bathing rituals were made by married Jewish women below the age of menopause, during initiation ceremonies and on the eve of the Sabbath.

# Georgian bathing

In the early nineteenth century, highlighted by the novels of Jane Austen, wealthy Georgians travelled to mineral spa towns such as the English city of Bath to 'take the waters', where they were also able to pamper themselves with other beauty treatments. At home servants would supply them with warmed water to wash themselves from a basin in their chambers.

For the average worker, dirt was a sign of their trade and their status. Blacksmiths, leather tanners, chimney sweeps and most ordinary people lived most of their lives covered in dirt. As none of their contemporaries washed regularly, the stench of their body odour went undetected – if everyone was smelly no one noticed.

# Victorian bathing

From the late Georgian period and into the Victorian era, wealthy people began to bathe for pleasure and recreational bathing increased with the construction of the new railway network. People could easily take a trip to the seaside where there were horse-drawn bathing machines, which wheeled them into the water to discreetly bathe, albeit fully clothed from head to toe in heavy bathing costumes.

With the introduction of plumbing, running hot water for bathing at home began to appear around the mid-nineteenth century, but only in the most aristocratic English residences. By the turn of the twentieth century many homes had bathrooms and people found that bathing could help limit the spread of disease.

# Finnish saunas

With at least 1,000 years of history, the traditional sauna is an ancient form of bathing from Finland. A small room or wooden hut heated to approximately 176°F (80°C), it is used for mental and physical relaxation as well as for bathing. The bather washes or showers with cold water, enters the sauna for a few minutes, then has another refreshing cold shower. This process is repeated several times. The Finnish sauna is similar to the Turkish 'hamam', the Native American 'inipi', the Russian 'banya' and the Japanese 'onsen'.

*Heating the water in this traditional sauna in Salmela, Finland, built 1910–1912.*

# Basic techniques

# Equipment, ingredients and moulds

To make the recipes in this book you will not need any complicated equipment; in fact, most of the equipment that you need you will probably have in your kitchen already. You will, however, need to purchase the raw ingredients to make your bath bombs, which are easily obtained from the growing number of mail order 'soap supplies' or 'bath bomb supplies' companies. These suppliers will usually sell most, or all, of the ingredients and moulds that you will need to make a bath bomb for craft and hobby use (see our list of suggested stockists on pages 144–147).

**To make the recipes in this book you will need the following:**

1 Plastic or glass bowl
2 Sieve
3 A 1 cup measure (or weighing scales)
4 Set of teaspoon and tablespoon measures
5 A clean kitchen surface, tray, greaseproof or baking paper
6 Small spray or spritz bottle filled with water
7 Moulds
8 Citric acid
9 Bicarbonate of soda
10 Fragrance or essential oils (optional)
11 Colour (optional)
12 Herbs and additives (optional)
13 Cardboard box for storage

Store bath bombs in a cardboard box, an airtight plastic container, or wrap in acid-free tissue paper or a plastic bag. Do not store in metal containers as the bath bombs might react with the metal.

The basic equipment and ingredients needed to make your own bath bombs.

# Finding moulds

Many household objects or packaging from everyday life can be re-used as bath bomb moulds. Basically, you can use any plastic container to make bath bombs providing that they do not have sharp corners as these can be difficult to turn out. Use your imagination and make use of the things that may otherwise be thrown away.

**Here are some of the household items used for moulds in this book:**

1   Tennis ball cut in half (use a serrated knife and, holding firmly, very carefully cut through the ball)
2   Plastic wine glasses or cups
3   Plastic plant pot holders
4   Empty plastic yoghurt pots or food containers
5   Ice cube moulds for mini bath bombs (the flexible, rubbery ones are best)
6   Cardboard or polystyrene packaging for apple storage from your local supermarket (these are good for placing your bath bombs in for drying)

### Tip

*Children's clay toy sets and plastic packaging from toys with indentations also make excellent moulds.*

*A selection of moulds found around the home.*

# Ready-made moulds

Most ingredients and moulds can be purchased from the many internet-based soap or bath bomb ingredient suppliers (see pages 144–147 for details). Round, heart and other shaped moulds specifically for bath bomb use can be purchased or soap-making moulds can also be used.

Soap-making moulds usually come with several moulds on a sheet; these are often plain shapes such as hearts, or rectangles, but there are also many fun themed moulds such as animals, shells, or seasonal shapes.

If you have purchased a sheet of moulds, you will need to carefully cut out a single shape for use as a bath bomb mould to be turned out flat on to your surface.

Other fun moulds can be found at craft supply shops and from chocolate-making suppliers; again there are usually a few on a sheet so you will need to carefully cut out a single mould.

*A selection of ready-made, purchased moulds.*

# The basic bath bomb recipe

**Use this basic recipe for making all the individual variations on pages 82–141. Once you have mastered it you can adapt and create your own bespoke bath bombs.**

## Ingredients

300g (11oz or 1 cup) granulated citric acid
600g (1lb 5oz or 2 cups) bicarbonate of soda (baking soda)
1 teaspoon essential oil or fragrance oil
1 teaspoon herbs, glitter and/or liquid colour
5g (approx 0.2oz or 1 teaspoon) oil or melted butter
Binder – water, witch hazel or floral water in a spritz or spray bottle

### Alternative recipe

If you want to make more economical bath bombs you can use one part granular citric acid to three parts bicarbonate of soda (baking soda); however, we recommend using the quantities stated in the basic recipe above if you are using oils or butters (as these ingredients may lessen the fizz in your bomb).

# Making the mixture

**1** First measure out the citric acid into the bowl.

**2** Measure out the bicarbonate of soda into a sieve sitting on your bowl and sieve the ingredients on top of the citric acid.

**3** Make a well with your fingers and add any dry ingredients, e.g. herbs, glitter, etc.

**4** Now sprinkle in your colour and fragrance; the mixture may fizz when you add liquid colour. This is quite normal, just cover the fizzing colour with some dry ingredients.

**5** Start mixing all of the ingredients together with your hands (do not use bare hands if you have any cuts or sores as it will sting).

**6** Make sure that ALL of the colour and fragrance is thoroughly mixed; occasionally the colour may clump into little blobs so you will need to make sure that all of the colour has been incorporated evenly.

**7**

To distribute any clumps of colour, try rubbing the mixture between the palms of your hands.

**NOTE: Once your ingredients are weighed out, do not leave the mixture to sit as it may start to set by itself without even adding any liquid.**

**8**

Now for the tricky part – binding the mixture together. If you are using an oil or butter add this now to your mixture (for instructions on melting butters see page 31).

**9**

Next, using your spray bottle, spray several times with water (you can also use witch hazel or floral waters) onto your mixture and mix in with your hands. When the water reacts with the ingredients the mixture will become icy cold and heavy to the touch. Squeeze the mixture together with your hands before adding more water.

**10**

If you do not have a spritz bottle you can dampen your hands under a tap, or dip your fingers into a small bowl of water, and sprinkle a little water into the mixture from your finger tips. However, there is a danger of adding in too much water.

**11**

Your mixture should resemble damp sand and should hold together well when squeezed in your fist. If your mixture is too wet, when you turn it out it can 'grow' and change shape. If it is dry and crumbles, add some more water. When you are happy with your mix, mould your bath bombs fairly quickly so that the mixture does not start to dry out. If it does dry out, just spritz on some water.

**NOTE: If using oil or melted butter in your recipe it will also act as a binder so you will not need to spritz as much water. This will also depend on how much fragrance or extra dry ingredients you have used, or even the humidity on the day of making.**

# Moulding (using a round mould)

**1**

If you are making a round bath bomb, take both halves of your mould and scoop in the mixture, slightly over-filling each side with mixture, and press both sides together firmly. To make both sides stick together you will need to press and grind from side to side slightly.

**2**

Gently remove the top half of the mould, whilst holding the bottom half in the other hand.

**3**

Using the corner of the empty half of the mould, remove the excess mixture from around the outside of the bomb.

**NOTE:** If you are not sure about unmoulding the whole bomb, and you have enough moulds, you can leave the bath bombs in the bottom half of each mould for an hour until they are slightly set, making it easier to unmould the whole bomb. However, don't leave them for too long as they will be difficult to remove.

Place the exposed side of the bath bomb in the palm of your hand, and gently remove the other half of the mould.

Now very carefully place the whole bath bomb on an apple storage tray, or on an old towel. This will prevent the bottoms of the bath bombs from becoming too indented with the pressure of sitting on a flat surface.

Leave your moulded bath bombs overnight to set and the next day they will be ready to use. Make sure they are kept out of reach from children and pets.

Now the really important part. Run yourself a warm bath, turn down the lights, pour yourself a drink, put on some relaxing music, climb in to your warm bath and pop in one of your own, delicately blended, aromatic, hand-crafted, hand-moulded bath bombs. Sink into the water knowing that you are partaking in an age-old ritual to relax the mind, body and spirit, allowing your skin to soften and hydrate and your muscles to relax in the soothing, fragrant water.

# Using other shaped moulds
## How to mould a flat or patterned bath bomb

**1** With one hand, scoop up some of the mixture and place it in to the bath bomb mould held in the other hand.

**2** Press the mixture firmly into the detail on your bath bomb mould and around the sides.

**3** Brush away any excess mixture, so that the mixture inside the mould is level with the outside of the mould.

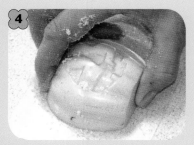

**4** With a swift motion, firmly place or lightly bang your mould on to a kitchen surface, a piece of greaseproof paper, baking sheet, or a tray.

**5** Gently lift off the mould; you may need to gently sway the mould from side to side whilst lifting the mould upwards at the same time.

Leave your moulded bath bomb where it is, do not move it or touch it, otherwise it will crumble and fall apart. If it is a warm day, you may find that you can gently move the bath bomb from its position after a few hours, but you will need to leave it approximately 24 hours to fully dry out.

## Making a bath bomb with petals or herbs at the bottom

Bath bombs can look attractive with a few herbs on the top of the bomb, which will float around in the bath tub.

## Mini bath bombs in ice cube trays

A perfect way to make mini bath bombs is using an ice cube tray.

Take a small pinch of herbs such as rose petals, lavender buds or calendula petals and place them on the bottom of your mould. You will need fewer petals than you think.

Take your mixture and press firmly into each cavity. Leave to set hard overnight.

Add some mixture to the mould on top of the petals, press firmly, brush away the excess mixture with your hand so that the mixture is level and turn out onto your surface as before. Leave to dry for 24 hours.

The next day turn your mould over and press each bath bomb gently from the back of the mould, catching them with the other hand as they pop out. Several mini bath bombs at a time can be used in the bath.

## How to melt butters

If you are using melted butters such as shea, mango, cocoa or Monoi de Tahiti, place the weighed ingredients in a metal dish or mini saucepan and very gently, on a low heat, melt the butter. They will melt very quickly, particularly the Monoi, so do not leave them unattended as you do not want to overheat the oil and lose all of their wonderful properties. Once the butter has melted, leave it for a minute or two to cool before adding to the ingredients.

**NOTE: If you are using a metal bowl or dish with a metal handle, such as the one in the picture, remember to use an oven glove or tea towel as the handle will be hot.**

## How to mix two colours together

Although slightly fiddly, splitting your mixture in two and colouring each half differently can make an attractive bath bomb. For some of the recipes in this book we divide the mixture in two, colour each half, and put the two colours in the same mould. Turn out and leave to set as before. The resulting bath bomb is then a pretty two-tone of colour.

# Troubleshooting

There is no such thing as a failed bath bomb, only beautifully made fizzing bath dust or effervescing rocks.

### Does your bath bomb look dry and crumbly?

If so, you have probably not added enough water. Fear not, pop all of the crumbly mixture into a plastic bag, beat gently with a rolling pin and you have made some fizzing bath dust.

### Has your bath bomb erupted?

You have probably added too much water. Beat gently with a rolling pin and you have designed the latest aromatic 'cosmic moon rocks'.

### Scared of turning out your bombs?

If you do not have the confidence to turn out your bath bomb, you can leave your mixture sitting in the mould overnight and turn out the bath bombs the next day. You will need to make sure that you have plenty of moulds to fill.

# Basic ingredients

# Essential oils

## What are essential oils?

Essential oils are the natural volatile liquids found in tiny amounts in aromatic plants, leaves, fruit, seeds, roots, wood, resin, gum, grasses and flowers which are produced by the plant to either protect itself against bacteria or fungus, or to attract insects for pollination. Although not actually oils as such, these concentrated aromatic compounds are highly fragrant and carry the distinctive 'essential' scent, or essence, of the plant.

## Aromatherapy

Aromatherapy is a form of complementary therapy that applies essential oils in several ways such as massage, inhalation, vaporization, compresses, bath products and skincare to help ease a multitude of health complaints and conditions, while at the same time affecting the emotions and wellbeing.

Throughout history most cultures have highly valued the therapeutic effects of aromatic plant oils, with ancient Egypt perhaps the most well known, attracting physicians from all corners of the globe to learn plant medicine from their experts. More recently, in the 1920s French chemist René-Maurice Gattefossé accidentally discovered the healing and antiseptic properties of essential oils upon burning his arm and cooling it with the nearest substance available which was lavender. After experiencing the relief of his pain, and in particular the speedy healing of his arm, he spent his life researching the subject and was the first to use the term 'aromathérapie'. In 1964 a fellow Frenchman, Dr Jean Valnet, further researched these healing properties on wounded soldiers and published his well-known aromatherapist's bible *The Practice of Aromatherapy*.

As we know, our olfactory sense (our sense of smell) can trigger changes in our moods – a stroll in a fragrant rose garden can lift and calm the spirits, whilst a walk down a dirty alley way with smelly garbage cans can give us an unpleasant feeling, thereby lowering the spirits. The aroma of essential oils is believed to have the same effect on our mood.

A warm bath is one of the best ways of using essential oils as the complex chemical compounds found in the essential oils are said to enter the bloodstream through the skin. The blissful sensation of submerging your body in warm aromatic water is also one of the most effective ways of unwinding and letting go of the day's tensions and stresses.

# Some therapeutic uses of essential oils

Essential oils are known to have different therapeutic benefits and have been reported to be of great help in easing various skin conditions. **Oils must not be used directly on the skin and should be used in a carrier oil, bath bomb, soap or cream.**

| | |
|---|---|
| **Dry skin** | geranium, rose geranium, rose, sandalwood, chamomile, neroli, ylang ylang, palmarosa and patchouli |
| **Ageing and mature skin** | rose, neroli, frankincense, myrrh, patchouli, lavender, palmarosa, geranium, rose geranium and sandalwood |
| **Oily skin** | lemon, bergamot, juniper, lime, geranium, cypress, rose geranium, mandarin, orange, sandalwood, neroli, cedarwood and lavender |
| **Sensitive skin** | rose, chamomile, lavender, neroli, rose and sandalwood |
| **Fungal infections such as athlete's foot or ringworm** | manuka, pine, lemon and tea tree |
| **Eczema or dermatitis** | bergamot, cedarwood, geranium, chamomile, lavender and sandalwood |
| **Stretch marks and scars** | frankincense, geranium, lavender, neroli, patchouli and rose |
| **PMT and painful periods** | basil, clary sage, cypress, frankincense, geranium, rose geranium, grapefruit, neroli, chamomile, jasmine, lavender, rose and marjoram |
| **Muscle aches** | basil, coriander, cypress, eucalyptus, ginger, grapefruit, juniper, lavender, marjoram, black pepper, pine, rosemary, sage and vetiver |
| **Anxiety, depression or stress** | basil, bergamot, chamomile, clary sage, frankincense, lavender, cypress, mandarin, marjoram, neroli, orange, palmarosa, rose, vetiver, jasmine and ylang ylang |

*Basic ingredients*

# How are essential oils obtained?

It can take a huge amount of raw material to obtain even a small amount of essential oil, so large areas of crops are needed for the purpose of extracting the precious, volatile oils. Different extraction methods are used to obtain the essential oils of plants which are held in special cells within the plant tissues.

## Steam distillation

Most essential oils from flowers or leaves are obtained through steam distillation. The steam softens the plant material releasing the essential oil into the water vapour. The fragrant vapour is passed along a pipe to a condenser where it is cooled back into water. The oil floats to the surface and is skimmed off, filtered and packaged.

## Expression

Essential oil from citrus fruit is stored in the large cells in the coloured outer rind, or peel, close to the surface of the fruit. In the past, expression was carried out by the sponge method where the citrus peel was soaked in water, and then compressed against a sponge to collect the oil which was then squeezed out and collected.

These days most citrus oils are produced by machine abrasion, where the outer peel of the fruit is scarified and removed by machine, the loose material is then removed by water and fed into a large centrifugal separator machine, which spins the essential oil out of the rind.

## Solvent extraction

The aromas of some flowers such as jasmine, mimosa, hyacinth and tuberose are destroyed by heat and therefore require different methods to extract the oil. In days gone by, the famous French perfume-making area of Grasse used a process called 'enfleurage' whereby glass plates in a frame called a chassis, were covered with purified fat on which the freshly picked flowers were placed and left to infuse. After a few days, the old petals were removed and replaced with fresh ones until the fat became completely saturated with the essential oil from the flowers. The resulting 'pomade' was mixed with alcohol to separate the essential oil from the fat and once the alcohol evaporated the essential oil was left. The separated fragrant fat was then often used in the manufacture of soap.

Nowadays, a solvent such as hexane or alcohol is poured over the fragile petals, the solvent penetrates the plant tissue and the essential oil dissolves into the solvent along with other material from the plant such as chlorophyll, waxes and other resinous matter. The resulting concentrated oily substance known as a 'concrete' is then purified into an 'absolute'. Absolutes are used more in perfumery than aromatherapy as the solvent extraction process produces a substance which has a closer aroma to the original plant than an essential oil.

## Carbon dioxide extraction ($CO_2$)

The latest extraction method involves using a gas such as carbon dioxide under very high pressure. Although this method is expensive it yields a good quality oil with no solvents being left, or reacting with the 'essence', which is the case when using hexane or alcohol in solvent extraction methods.

# Safety

Essential oils should not be taken internally and must be kept away from children and animals. If oils are accidentally swallowed, seek medical help immediately. If you get any essential oils in the eye area, irrigate with water immediately and if symptoms persist contact medical advice. Although essential oils (aromatherapy oils) have been historically used to ease medical conditions, they must in no way be substituted for medical advice.

Most essential oils should not be used neat on the body. Essential oils are very potent and only a small amount of oils are used in bath products; we therefore advise that the amounts stated in our recipes should not be exceeded.

Most essential oils should be avoided by young children, except where indicated in a recipe that they are suitable for children, such as lavender, chamomile and mandarin. The recipes in this book are therefore intended for adults (over 16 years) unless specified otherwise. Essential oils in recipes can always be adapted, and a fragrance oil can be used as a substitute. None of the recipes in this book are intended for use by children under the age of six. If you suffer from allergies, we advise doing a test patch before immersing your whole body in the bath water.

Essential oils from some citrus fruits can be phototoxic – orange, lemon, grapefruit, bergamot, pettigrain, lime and mandarin can react with sunlight, so it is best to avoid direct exposure from sunlight or UV light approximately 12 hours after using.

## Advice from a qualified practitioner or medical adviser should be sought if you:

- have a known medical condition such as high blood pressure or epilepsy
- are receiving any psychiatric or medical treatment
- take homeopathic or herbal remedies
- are pregnant or breast-feeding
- wish to treat young children

# Storage

Essential oils should be stored in dark-coloured glass jars or bottles in a cool environment. Many oils can last for years if stored in this way; however, citrus oils will generally lose their properties after approximately one year after purchase. As with perfumes, exposure to oxygen will also quickly degrade essential oils so it is best to make sure that there is as little space between the surface of the oil and the top of the bottle as possible. Essential oils can also damage clothing and wooden surfaces so we would recommend covering yourself and your surfaces before using essential oils.

*Store essential oils in dark-coloured bottles in a cool place.*

# Directory of some common essential oils

There are too many essential oils to list in this book so here is a selection of the most common and readily available oils and descriptions of each. You will find a letter after the name of each essential oil which denotes whether the oil is a top **(T)**, middle **(M)** or base note **(B)**.

**(T, M)** indicates that this is a top to middle note and can be used as either. The perfume and fragrance section on page 51 will teach you about top, middle and base notes and how to blend your own therapeutic perfume for use in your bath bombs.

## Basil (T)
*Ocimum basilicum*
**Fragrance:** a light, fresh, green and sweet scent with a balsamic undertone.
**Known uses:** nervous tension and indigestion, memory, headache, migraine, respiratory complaints, colds, concentration, periods. Caution: use in moderation – at not more than 2% as can cause sensitive skin.
**Blends with:** geranium, hyssop, bergamot, black pepper, cedarwood, fennel, ginger, grapefruit, lavender, lemon, marjoram, neroli and verbena.

*Fresh basil*

## Bergamot (T)
*Citrus bergamia*
**Fragrance:** sweet, fresh, green, bright and citrus scent with a warm floral quality.
**Known uses:** uplifting the spirits, stress, depression, boosting immunity, colds and flu, thrush, urinary tract infection. Bergamot is a small bitter orange from Lombardy in Italy, best known for its flavouring of Earl Grey tea, and is one of the main ingredients in Eau-de-Cologne. Strongly phototoxic, use sparingly, maximum usage 0.4%.
**Blends with:** jasmine, cypress, neroli, lavender, black pepper, clary sage, frankincense, geranium, mandarin, nutmeg, orange, rosemary, sandalwood, vetiver and ylang ylang.

## Black Pepper (M)
*Piper nigrum*
**Fragrance:** fresh, warm, musty, sharp, spicy and dry-woody smell.
**Known uses:** digestion, colds and flu, immune system, circulation, cellulite, aches, pains, rheumatism, relaxing muscles, aphrodisiac. One of the oldest known spices and known to have been used in India over 4,000 years ago. Not recommended in concentrations of more than 0.5%.
**Blends with:** sandalwood, frankincense, juniper, rosemary, cardamom, fennel, cedarwood, ginger, bergamot, neroli, bergamot, clary sage, clove, coriander, geranium, grapefruit, lavender, lemon, lime, mandarin, sage and ylang ylang.

## Cardamom (M)

*Elettaria cardamomum*

**Fragrance:** warm, fruity, sweet and spicy aromatic scent with a pungent freshness and woody, floral undertones.

**Known uses:** digestion, nausea, heartburn, coughs, flatulence, bad breath caused by gastric problems, mental fatigue, aphrodisiac and a general tonic. Related botanically to ginger, it has been used in traditional Chinese and Indian Ayurvedic medicine for over 3,000 years and is used today in Eastern medicinal practise as a tonic for the lungs and for its immune-boosting properties.

**Blends with:** rose, rosemary, frankincense, sandalwood, ylang ylang, bergamot, cinnamon, cloves, caraway and cedarwood.

## Cedarwood (B)

*Cedrus atlantica* or *Juniperus virginiana*

**Fragrance:** clean-smelling, sharp and fresh with slightly sweet, woody, balsamic undertones.

**Known uses:** acne, arthritis, rheumatism, bronchitis, nervous tension, eczema, oily skin, cystitis and urinary infections. A native tree of North America, the oil is distilled from wood chips and sawdust and was used historically in medicine by the Native Americans. The Egyptians are known to have used the oil as an insect repellent and in mummification.

**Blends with:** bergamot, cinnamon, cypress, frankincense, jasmine, juniper, lavender, lemon, neroli, myrrh, sandalwood, vetiver, rose and rosemary.

## Chamomile (Roman) (M)

*Anthemis nobilis*

**Fragrance:** refreshing, sweet, herbaceous, apple-like, fresh scent.

**Known uses:** widely used in baby and children's products. Anti-inflammatory, menstrual cramps, insomnia, migraine, PMS, restlessness, stress, allergies. This soothing and calming oil is pale blue in colour and is known as 'ground apple' and said to be beneficial to those with hay fever (unless you have an allergy to ragweed).

**Blends with:** clary sage, bergamot, lavender, geranium, jasmine, tea tree, grapefruit, rose, lemon, ylang ylang, marjoram and rose geranium.

## Clary Sage (T, M)

*Salvia sclarea*

**Fragrance:** sweet, nutty, rich, herbaceous.

**Known uses:** muscle relaxant, depression, menstrual cramps, stress, nervous tension, insomnia, aphrodisiac. Do not use during pregnancy or when drinking alcohol as it can make you drowsy.

**Blends with:** juniper, lavender, sandalwood, coriander, geranium, jasmine, lemon, rose, pine, frankincense and citrus oils.

*Cardamom pods*

*Dried Chamomile flowers*

*Clary sage*

Bath Bombs

## Cypress (M)

*Cupressus sempervirens*

**Fragrance:** earthy, fresh and green, smoky and nutty with a slight spiciness and sweet, resinous notes.

**Known uses:** spasmodic coughs, bronchitis, lymphatic drainage, detoxifying, cellulite, water retention, soothes emotions, varicose veins, haemorrhoids, circulation and chilblains. Historically used as an incense ingredient and in aftershaves and colognes.

**Blends with:** juniper, pine, bergamot, clary sage, lavender, marjoram, sandalwood, rosemary, frankincense and all the citrus oils.

## Eucalyptus (T)

*Eucalyptus globulus*

**Fragrance:** strong medicinal, sharp, fresh, camphoraceous smell with slight woody undertones.

**Known uses:** not used much in perfumery but historically used as a medicinal herb in Australia by Aborigines. Fevers, colds, bronchitis, rheumatism, muscular aches and pains, urinary and genital infections. Caution: must not be swallowed.

**Blends with:** cypress, lavender, marjoram, cedarwood, lemongrass, tea tree, lemon, thyme and pine.

## Frankincense (B)

*Boswellia carterii*

**Fragrance:** fresh top note when first smelt, with sweet, woody, resinous undertones.

**Known uses:** meditation, stress, anti-inflammatory, damaged or ageing skin, toning, rejuvenating, anxiety, tension, mucus conditions, i.e., coughs, bronchitis, laryngitis. A highly prized gum resin, used as far back as the ancient Egyptians for skincare and in incense for worship and fumigation of the sick – also known as Olibanum.

**Blends with:** basil, neroli, pine, sandalwood, myrrh, cedarwood, vetiver, lavender, orange, bergamot and lemon.

## Geranium (T, M)

*Pelargonium graveolens*

**Fragrance:** fresh, rosy, sweet floral with a hint of lemon and fresh green.

**Known uses:** neuralgia, anxiety, depression, sedative, uplifting, diuretic, dry and inflamed skin, hot flushes, oily skin, skin toner and tonic. Widely used in perfumery and skincare.

**Blends with:** any oil, particularly basil, bergamot, marjoram, palmarosa, rose, sandalwood, cedarwood, clary sage, grapefruit, jasmine, lavender, lime, neroli, orange and rosemary.

## Ginger (T, M)

*Zingiber officinale*

**Fragrance:** hot, dry, pungent and musty, with a lingering spicy sweetness.

**Known uses:** colds and flu, fevers, immune system, poor circulation, muscular pains, nausea, aphrodisiac. Ginger root has been traditionally used in Chinese medicine for digestion and circulation.

**Blends with:** all citrus and spicy oils and in particular bergamot, frankincense, neroli, rose, sandalwood, ylang ylang, vetiver, juniper and cedarwood.

*Eucalyptus leaves*

*Ginger root*

## Grapefruit (T)
*Citrus grandis*

**Fragrance:** fresh, green, zesty, sweet and citrus smell.

**Known uses:** detoxifying, tonic, oily skin, acne, cellulite, insomnia, constipation, digestive, liver and kidney problems, hangovers, immune system, colds and influenza. A good pick-me-up with a positive effect on the mind. Caution: can be phototoxic.

**Blends with:** bergamot, palmarosa, pine, frankincense, geranium, eucalyptus and pine.

## Jasmine (M, B)
*Jasminum officinale*

**Fragrance:** rich, warm, sweet, exotic floral scent.

**Known uses:** anxiety, depression, dry and sensitive skin, aphrodisiac, labour pains, post-natal depression, menstrual pain. Because of its importance in the perfume industry, jasmine is known as the 'King of Oils', the name deriving from the Arabic *yasmin*. The flowers are picked at night, when they are one day old.

**Blends with:** bergamot, sandalwood, rose and all citrus oils.

## Juniper (M)
*Juniperus communis*

**Fragrance:** fresh, warm, pungent, camphoraceous, woody, herbaceous smell.

**Known uses:** detox, digestion, urinary tract, diuretic, respiratory complaints, concentration, rheumatism, gout, circulation, oily skin, acne. Juniper berries are used in the production of gin.

**Blends with:** cedarwood, bergamot, cypress, rose, ginger, sandalwood, lavender, pine, rosemary and all citrus oils.

## Lavender (T, M)
*Lavandula angustifolia*

**Fragrance:** fresh, light, soft, clean sweet and floral.

**Known uses:** an extremely useful oil and the most widely used for its numerous therapeutic benefits which are too many to list here. The most common uses being for: stress, nervous tension, pain, insomnia, headaches, neuralgia, eczema, psoriasis, thrush, wounds, burns, stings, bites, shock and repelling insects. The Romans used lavender to bathe and the word 'lavender' is derived from their word for bathing 'lavare'. Widely used in perfumery, lavender blends well with many other essential oils, and as the most versatile it must be the number one choice for every first aid kit.

**Blends with:** all oils.

## Lemon (T)
*Citrus medica limonum*

**Fragrance:** fresh, sweet, green, citrus smell.

**Known uses:** tonic, diuretic, digestion, colds, flu, arthritis, immune system, lymphatic drainage, concentration, oily skin, rheumatism, gout, abscesses, boils, acne, high blood pressure, varicose veins and circulation. Caution: phototoxic.

**Blends with:** lavender, rose, sandalwood, eucalyptus, geranium, juniper and neroli.

*Fresh lavender flowers*

*Jasmine flowers*

## Lemongrass (T, M)

*Cymbopogon schoenanthus* or *Cymbopogon citratus*

**Fragrance:** citrus, herbaceous, fresh, sweet, zesty scent.

**Known uses:** tonic, digestion, migraine, respiratory conditions, fever, muscular aches and pains, constipation, depression, anxiety, nervous exhaustion, stress, athlete's foot, acne, jet lag, pick-me-up, hangovers, repelling insects such as fleas, ticks and lice in pets. A fast-growing perennial grass from India, locally known as 'choomana poolu', used in Ayurvedic medicine to help cool fevers and to treat infectious diseases. Caution: phototoxic.

**Blends with:** basil, geranium, rosemary, tea tree, vetiver, cedarwood, coriander, jasmine, lavender, pine, eucalyptus, neroli, palmarosa, rosemary and tea tree.

## Lime (T)

*Citrus aurantifolia*

**Fragrance:** fresh, green, sharp and zesty citrus peel aroma.

**Known uses:** astringent, tonic, headaches, fevers, immune system, flu, bronchitis, sinusitis, clearing the mind, oily skin, acne, depression, circulation, cellulite, obesity, travel sickness, arthritis and rheumatism. Caution: phototoxic.

**Blends with:** juniper, neroli, lavender, clary sage, ylang ylang and citrus oils.

## Mandarin (T)

*Citrus nobilis*

**Fragrance:** very sweet, rich, tangy, zesty and floral scent.

**Known uses:** restless children with tantrums, stress, stretch marks, nervous indigestion, oily skin, digestion, stomach cramps, flatulence, diarrhoea, constipation, circulation, fluid retention, insomnia. One of the most gentle oils, mandarin can be used by children, during pregnancy and for the elderly. May be slightly phototoxic.

**Blends with:** chamomile, lavender, frankincense, juniper, bergamot, clary sage, lavender, nutmeg and neroli.

## Marjoram (M)

*Origanum marjorana*

**Fragrance:** warm, woody, slightly spicy, soft and sweet aroma.

**Known uses:** muscular aches, insomnia, sedative, digestion, PMT, hypertension, rheumatism, arthritis, colds, bronchitis, migraine, nervous indigestion. The name 'Origanum' comes from the Greek language, meaning 'joy of the mountains'.

**Blends with:** lavender, bergamot, ginger, vetiver, cypress, cedarwood, chamomile, eucalyptus and tea tree.

## Manuka (T, M)

*Leptosperum scoparium*

**Fragrance:** a sweet honey-like aroma, with woody, mossy notes.

**Known uses:** research has shown similar anti-bacterial, anti-fungal and anti-inflammatory properties as tea tree but there is evidence to suggest that it is up to 20 times more effective, less sensitizing and has a more pleasing aroma. Manuka is known to be highly bactericidal and insecticidal with a wide variety of uses such as for cuts, spots, boils, ulcers, stress, anxiety, nervous tension, dry and sensitive skin. The effect of manuka is so powerful that it has now been introduced into hospitals to fight superbugs. Although a relatively new oil in the modern practice of aromatherapy, manuka oil has been used historically by the Maori people of New Zealand as a medicinal herb.

**Blends with:** bergamot, black pepper, cedarwood, ginger, juniper, lavender, peppermint, rose, rosemary, sandalwood, vetiver and ylang ylang.

*A fresh lime*

## Neroli (Orange Blossom) (T, M)

*Citrus aurantium*

**Fragrance:** exquisite floral, sweet scent. Citrus-like with rich, soft green undertones. Light and refreshing.

**Known uses:** tones and rejuvenates the complexion, particularly dry, mature skin, wrinkles and stretch marks. Helps scar tissue, wounds, cuts, eases nervous indigestion and irritable bowel symptoms. Uplifting, relaxing, eases panic, insomnia, vertigo, shock and sudden emotional upsets.

**Blends with:** citrus oils, clary sage, jasmine, lavender, geranium, sandalwood and ylang ylang.

## Orange (Sweet) (T)

*Citrus aurantium dulcis or sinensis*

**Fragrance:** sweet, fresh, fruity smell.

**Known uses:** slow digestion, liver, constipation, tonic, digestion, nervous indigestion, depression, tension headaches, cellulite, detoxing, obesity, immune system, stress, colds, influenza. A happy and warming oil which helps to relax children at bedtime.

**Blends with:** peppermint, black pepper, ginger, frankincense, sandalwood, vetiver and lavender.

*Marjoram*

## Patchouli (B)

*Pogostemon cablin*

**Fragrance:** aromatic, woody and musky with spicy, musty, earthy-sweet undertones.

**Known uses:** depression, scars, stretch marks, acne, skin conditioner for dry, cracked or ageing skin, eczema, antiseptic, aphrodisiac. Historically used in the fabric of Indian shawls and linen to protect them from moths.

**Blends with:** bergamot, rose, rose geranium, clary sage, geranium, lavender, chamomile, cedarwood and myrrh.

## Palmarosa (M)

*Cymbopogon martini*

**Fragrance:** soft, sweet, rosy, floral with gentle notes of lemon.

**Known uses:** stress, anxiety, nervous tension, calming, uplifting, improving appetite, antiseptic, acne, eczema, urinary tract, diarrhoea, skincare. An aromatic grass with a similar, but much less expensive, fragrance to rose, and thus widely used in perfumery.

**Blends with:** bergamot, geramium, sandalwood, orange, grapefruit, chamomile, rosemary, lime and ylang ylang.

## Petitgrain (T, M)

*Citrus aurantium*

**Fragrance:** fresh, green, floral smell with a hint of citrus and woody undertones.

**Known uses:** stress, panic, nervous exhaustion, depression, digestion, stomach cramps, muscle spasms, calming, insomnia, greasy skin. Useful for convalescence, emotional conditions and a general pick-me-up. Petitgrain is distilled from the leaves and twigs of the bitter orange tree, whereas neroli is obtained from the flower of the same tree. Caution: phototoxic.

**Blends with:** juniper, clary sage, clove, lavender, rosemary, bergamot, orange, lemon, neroli, jasmine, palmarosa, sandalwood, chamomile, geranium and ylang ylang.

*Basic ingredients*

## Peppermint (T)

*Mentha piperita*

**Fragrance:** strong, fresh, minty aroma with sweet undertones.

**Known uses:** indigestion, nausea, stomach cramps, headache and migraine, concentration, muscle pains, colds, coughs, deodorant.

**Blends with:** rosemary, black pepper, ginger, eucalyptus, lavender, marjoram, lemon and rosemary.

## Pine (M)

*Pinus sylvestris*

**Fragrance:** fresh, forest smell with sweet, balsamic tones.

**Known uses:** urinary infection, diuretic, tonic, colds, flu, bronchitis, rheumatism, cystitis, muscular aches and pains, period pains, deodorizing and antiseptic.

**Blends with:** cedarwood, cypress, lemon, eucalyptus, marjoram, juniper, lavender and rosemary.

## Rose (M)

*Rosa damascena (Rose otto)* or *Rosa centifolia (Rose maroc)*

**Fragrance:** rich, deep, soft rosy-floral scent.

**Known uses:** nervous system, depression, PMT, infertility, aphrodisiac, menopause, antiseptic, toning, anti-inflammatory, tonic. A symbol of love and purity and known as the 'Queen of Flowers', roses have been used both aesthetically and medicinally for centuries, with the first rose oil reputedly made in Persia. It takes a huge amount of blooms just to make one drop of precious rose oil. Caution: this oil may cause skin irritation.

**Blends with:** geranium, jasmine, sandalwood, mandarin, neroli, frankincense and palmarosa.

## Rosemary (T, M)

*Rosmarinus officinalis*

**Fragrance:** strong, fresh, herbaceous, camphoraceous scent.

**Known uses:** muscular aches and pains, rheumatism, painful periods, circulation, headaches, concentration, sprains, lymphatic drainage, digestion, colds and flu. Used in incense, sick rooms and to drive away evil spirits.

**Blends with:** cedarwood, geranium, bergamot, basil, lavender, lemongrass and peppermint.

## Rose Geranium (T, M)

*Pelargonium graveolens* and *Pelargonium rosa*

**Fragrance:** fresh, crisp, sweet rosy scent.

**Known uses:** nervous system, PMT, anxiety, menopause, stress, eczema, lymphatic system, jaundice, haemorrhoids, gall stones and mild depression.

**Blends with:** basil, bergamot, lime, cedarwood, clary sage, grapefruit, lavender, jasmine, lemon, neroli, rosemary and orange.

*Rose geranium*

## Sandalwood (B)
*Santalum album*

**Fragrance:** soft, deep, rich, sweet, exotic and woody aroma.

**Known uses:** urinary and venereal infections, antiseptic, meditation, aphrodisiac, nervous exhaustion, eczema, chest infections, bronchitis, asthma, coughs and dry skin. Used since ancient times for incense, embalming and widely used in the perfume and cosmetics industry.

**Blends with:** bergamot, palmarosa, geranium, vetiver, ylang ylang, lavender, jasmine, cedarwood, rose, black pepper and myrrh.

## Tea Tree (M)
*Melaleuca alternifolia*

**Fragrance:** fresh, strong, spicy, pungent camphoraceous smell

**Known uses:** immune system, colds, influenza, anti-viral, anti-bacterial, anti-fungal, muscle aches and pains, shock, skin infections, genital infections, vaginal thrush, cystitis, herpes, bronchitis, asthma, coughs, sinusitis, tuberculosis, abscesses, acne, burns, oily skin, athlete's foot, ringworm, cold sores, blemishes, warts, sunburn. A native to Australia, tea tree has been used historically by the Aborigines as an antiseptic and for a variety of other medicinal purposes.

**Blends with:** clove, lavender, eucalyptus, rosemary, pine, lemon and thyme.

*Rose damascena*

## Vetiver (B)
*Vetiveria zizanoides*

**Fragrance:** heavy, sweet, earthy, warm, powerful, smoky scent with a woody, musty undertone.

**Known uses:** anti-depressant, aphrodisiac, insomnia, stress, circulation, anaemia, rheumatism, arthritis, muscular aches and pains, menstrual cramps, acne, wrinkles, stretch marks, mental and physical exhaustion. Vetiver is known as the 'oil of tranquillity' because of its deeply calming and relaxing properties.

**Blends with:** clary sage, lavender, jasmine, rose, sandalwood, patchouli and ylang ylang.

## Ylang Ylang (T, M)
*Cananga odorata*

**Fragrance:** intensely sweet, powerful, exotic, highly fragrant, floral scent with a creamy top note.

**Known uses:** stress, panic attacks, depression, anxiety, nervous conditions, aphrodisiac, high blood pressure, hyperpnoea, rapid breathing and heartbeat, impotence and frigidity, oily skin. The name means 'flower of flowers', and is spread on the beds of newlyweds in Indonesia. Use in moderation as too much can bring on a headache or nausea, just one or two drops may be enough. There are different grades of the oil from the distillation process, the first distillation being called ylang ylang 'extra' which has the sweetest odour and is used only for the perfume industry, the oil used in aromatherapy is a blend of the other grades of oil.

**Blends with:** sandalwood, jasmine, grapefruit, lavender, bergamot, cedarwood, jasmine, clary sage, lemon, rose, vetiver and sandalwood.

*Fresh rosemary*

*Basic ingredients*

# Perfume and fragrance

## The sense of smell

All organisms are able to identify chemical substances (odorant molecules) in their environment, which is essential to survival, and each has their own characteristic scent, which, although it may not be commonly apparent, is detected on a subconscious level.

We must be able to smell food that is decaying, danger such as fire or a gas leak and young mammals need their olfactory sense to detect mother's milk for feeding. Some scientists now believe that the selection process of a partner or mate may unknowingly involve our sense of smell via aromatic chemicals called pheromones.

Humans have approximately 1,000 different kinds of olfactory receptors and we can remember up to 10,000 different odours. This occurs when we breath in odorous molecules which travel up the nose, past olfactory receptor cells, where electrical signals are sent to the brain by nerve processes. This can instantly trigger very distinctive memories and associations from the past, a childhood trip, a relative, a place of worship, home, or other memories that were either pleasant or unpleasant experiences.

The human sense of smell (olfaction) has become weaker during evolution; we no longer need to negotiate our environment by our sense of smell as other animals do, or smell the scent of our enemy. We have fewer receptor cells than mice, but more than fish. Next time you look at your dog's nose twitching, you will know that his olfactory epithelium is around 40 times larger than yours, making his sense of smell up to several million times more powerful.

## What is perfume?

The word perfume (parfum) stems from the Latin *per* meaning 'through', and *fumum* meaning 'smoke'. Early perfumes were produced by burning materials such as wood, gums and resins to give a fragrant smoke (incense), which is still used in places of worship and for meditation today.

A perfume is a blend of fragrant essences and oils obtained from flowers, grasses, resin, bark, gum, fruit, animals and aroma chemicals, dissolved in an alcohol or oil base. Different amounts of these oils are mixed with varying grades of alcohol and water to produce certain strengths such as toilet water, eau de cologne, eau de toilette and the strongest and most expensive, eau de parfum and perfume. Perfumes (fragrances) are also used to scent cleaning products, candles, pot pourri, talc, creams, soaps, cosmetics and bath products.

Commercial perfumiers choose from thousands of natural essential oils and synthetic ingredients known as 'aroma chemicals' which are sourced from all corners of the globe. Used like the colours of an artist's pallet, many ingredients may be used in their formulations and complicated blends to produce olfactory masterpieces. The process of perfume blending is a highly skilful and complicated one, taking years of experience and training, requiring a particular 'nose' for the job. Just one drop of a precious ingredient added, and left to blend for several days with its counterparts, can literally make the difference between an ordinary and outstanding perfume.

# Perfume classifications

**Green** – ingredients such as galbanum, estragon, violet leaf and helional.

**Aldehydic** – a family of aroma chemicals known as aldehydes.

**Chypre (meaning 'cypress')** – warm and woody with oakmoss, amber or animalistic notes, patchouli, bergamot or rose.

**Citrus** – bergamot, lemon, lime, mandarin, orange and petitgrain

**Fougère (meaning 'fern')** – oakmoss, lavender, coumarin, herbaceous and woody. Mainly men's fragrances.

**Oriental** – floral, woody, amber and animal scents, camphoraceous oils and resins.

**Floral** – geranium, jasmine, neroli, rose, ylang ylang and lavender.

*Basic ingredients*

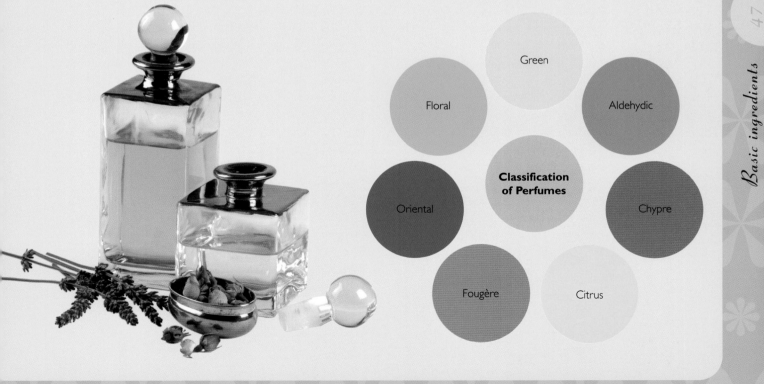

Green

Floral

Aldehydic

**Classification of Perfumes**

Oriental

Chypre

Fougère

Citrus

# The history of perfume

History shows us that for many centuries perfume has been an important part of life and ritual going back as far as the ancient Egyptians who were known to have used many fragranced preparations in their daily life. Scented flowers, woods and plants such as frankincense, myrrh, bitter almond and saffron were added to oil or fat and left to infuse in vases and pots. These aromatic oils were burned as incense during worship; used for animal sacrifice; embalming the dead; at festivals where guests' heads were anointed with oils; and in the coronation ceremonies of kings.

The most expensive perfumed oils were used by Egyptian society ladies for fashion and allurement as they bathed and moisturized their dry, sun-drenched skin. Queen Cleopatra was famously reputed to have used aromatic perfumes in abundance, not just for bathing, but also in the seduction of Mark Antony by adorning her ships with garlands of scented flowers and perfumes, the sea breeze trailing her arousing scent, leaving Mark Antony captivated by her sensual aroma.

In the past, not only were botanicals used in perfumery but some important base notes were originally derived from animals. The male musk deer from China and Tibet foraged on aromatic herbs in the high mountain ranges producing an extremely pungent secretion under its belly which we call 'musk'. Another animalistic base note, a glandular secretion called 'civet' was once sourced from civet cats. This foul-smelling substance, when combined with other ingredients in minute amounts, gave a perfume a new character and a surprisingly pleasing aroma. As with all animal-derived scents, civet is now an 'aroma chemical', synthetically reproduced and widely used in contemporary perfumery. Ambergris, or 'grey amber' is a grey, waxy substance from the sperm whale produced by its digestive system. A sweet, earthy marine-like scent with a strong faecal odour, it was expelled by dead or sick whales and found floating in the sea, or washed ashore. It was used as a fixative and base note in perfumery.

The first perfumiers and aromatherapists were priests, followed by physicians and medics, therefore in early history there was not always much distinction between perfumes and medicines as they were used for both purposes. However, over time, as trade routes increased and ingredients from around the world became more easily obtainable, perfumes developed and became more sophisticated and perfume 'shops' were opened.

Queen Elizabeth I of England was particularly fond of perfumes and, as was the fashion with the ladies of the era, enjoyed creating her own fragrances. She was often seen wearing fashionable perfumed gloves and carrying a pomander in her hand scented with rose water, benzoin, ambergris, civet, musk and other aromatic materials to prevent infection. At the time of her reign, perfumes were also burned in rooms and used to fragrance sheets, while scented bellows were puffed around the room to scent the air.

During the eighteenth century, heavier perfumes gave way to lighter ones such as the famous 'Eau de Cologne', an Italian recipe that was manufactured in Cologne, Germany, which changed the fashion of scents. (See page 55 to recreate this recipe.) This recipe was well loved by Napoleon who spent vast sums of money on expensive scents.

The perfume industry as we know it today was revolutionized in the southern region of France in a small town called Grasse. The 'capital of Provence' was originally an area for leather tanning, producing perfumed leather gloves which were all the rage in the seventeenth century. However, as the fashion for the gloves declined with the introduction of leather taxes, and with the birth of the industrial revolution, the perfume industry in Grasse took off and quickly grew.

In the nineteenth century, vast areas of fields were purchased by perfume companies and turned over to growing flowers such as jasmine, rose and tuberose, all hand-picked at certain times of the day. More perfume companies moved to the edge of town, which attracted other associated businesses such as the manufacturer of glass bottles and corks. Grasse became the market leaders in the supply of raw materials.

The advancement of chemical knowledge from the late nineteenth century onwards enabled perfumiers to create new scents using 'aroma chemicals', which replicate the more expensive and hard to find ingredients, such as animal scents, rose or violet. Essential oils and absolutes were therefore used less to add richness and sophistication to a perfume. The birth of new exciting 'aroma chemicals' gave perfumiers a much wider pallet to create designer scents that were unique and complex. Perfumes were therefore cheaper to produce making perfume more affordable for the masses, taking the perfume industry in the twentieth century to a new level, creating the multi-billion pound industry of today.

# Creating your own blends

Blending essential oils to create your own fragrance for use in the following bath bomb recipes does not have to be complicated. You can create your own fragrance blends from just a few ingredients.

It is important to note at this point that the following instructions are to enable you to create your own scent that can be used in bath bombs. These are NOT 'perfumes' or 'eau de toilettes' for spraying on the body, and as with all essential oils should *never* be used neat on the body or in the bath.

The perfume industry uses mostly aroma chemicals in their complex formulas, with essential oils only being used in small amounts to enhance the perfume. There are therefore little, or no therapeutic effects in most perfumes or fragrance oils. The instructions that follow will show you how to create your own essential oil blends which, using the practice of aromatherapy, may have therapeutic benefits.

You will, however, not be able to create your own fragrance oil using essential oils, so if you wish to have a flavour such as chocolate, apple, passionfruit, blueberry muffin, pina colada, mango, sea breeze etc., you will need to purchase a ready-made fragrance oil which has been produced with aroma chemicals (see suppliers list on page 144).

You could of course mix fragrance oils together to create different scents. For instance you could purchase a coconut fragrance oil and a pineapple fragrance oil and blend them together to make your own 'pina colada' fragrance. Or, you could blend together a few fruity fragrances to create your own 'fruit salad' fragrance oil. As mentioned before, these fragrance oils will not have any therapeutic benefits, they are purely for fun and aroma pleasure.

# Get to know your scents

First, become familiar with your essential oils and make sure that you keep notes of your findings, for if you create a stunning fragrance you will want to make sure that you know exactly how it was formulated.

When smelling an essential oil, do not put your nose directly over the top of the oil and vigorously sniff, otherwise you will get the full blast of the molecules up your nose and the scent will remain in the nostrils for some time making it very difficult for you to smell any more odours for some while.

Prepare some strips of paper (coffee filter bags are perfect) with which to blot some of the oil and waft the scent gently to and fro under your nose letting the fragrance lift upwards, and breath in slowly. You will usually only be able to sample around six scents at a time before you get nose fatigue.

If you decide to smell the scent directly from the bottle, it is important to note that you will not be getting the full aroma of the scent, to fully appreciate the aroma you should smell a scent from your paper testing strips as they can smell quite different once out of the bottle.

If your nose becomes overpowered, go outside to clear your nasal passages, or wave your hand under your nose to bring clear air into your nasal passages. If you have a cold, or if you smoke, this will impair your sense of smell. It is important to take breaks every so often as essential oils are highly concentrated and sampling them for long periods at a time may cause headaches or nausea. Our notes in the previous Essential oils section (see pages 38–45) will help you to describe the scents of your essential oil, but get used to writing down descriptions of the aromas that you experience. Blind testing yourself is always a useful and fun way of learning.

## Top, middle and base notes

Like a beautiful piece of music for your senses, the fragrant ingredients used to create perfumes are categorized by their 'notes'. A fragrance, or perfume, is made up of top, middle and base notes.

The **top notes**, or head notes, are small molecules and are the first 'notes' or 'smells' that you notice on sampling the fragrance. Assertive, bright and initially strong, they stimulate the senses and are important in creating the first impression of a fragrance. These volatile fresh, sharp top notes are powerful and intense to begin with, but are the first notes to disappear in a fragrance.

When the top notes begin to disappear, the **middle notes** start to come through and reveal themselves. These generally warm, soft and mellow oils provide the heart and body of your fragrance, rounding it off, and giving it complexity. They ease and pave the way for the next level of oils to emerge which, on their own, can be quite unpleasant, but with the partnership of the middle notes give support and durability.

The **base notes,** or 'theme', of the fragrance are usually heavy, exotic, intensely sensual and warm, they are generally woody, animalistic or resinous materials. These strong aromas will be the last scents to be detected, lingering the longest and 'fixing' the whole blend, holding the top and middle notes from evaporating too quickly.

| Top | | Middle | | Base |
|---|---|---|---|---|
| basil | lemongrass | black pepper | manuka | cedarwood |
| bergamot | lime | cardamom | neroli | frankincense |
| cardamom | mandarin | chamomile | palmrosa | jasmine |
| clary sage | neroli | clary sage | petitgrain | myrrh |
| cypress | orange (sweet) | geranium | pine | patchouli |
| eucalyptus | petitgrain | ginger | rose | sandalwood |
| geranium | peppermint | jasmine | rosemary | vetiver |
| ginger | pine | juniper | rose geranium | |
| grapefruit | rosemary | lavender | tea tree | |
| juniper | rose geranium | lemongrass | thyme | |
| lavender | ylang ylang | marjoram | ylang ylang | |
| lemon | | | | |

# Blending your perfume

Who has not been revived by the intoxicating scent of a rose garden, a walk through a citrus grove, or a visit to a herb garden? Decide on the theme of your essential oil blend, starting with the base, then the middle and finally the top notes (some people start from the top and work down, it is a personal choice).

Try and decide on one theme only for your therapeutic blend, and not a one-stop cure-all recipe, if you have back ache make a blend that will specifically target that complaint and not one that will also ease your hangover, PMT and athlete's foot all at the same time. Of course your therapeutic blend may help all of these things, but focus on one aspect at a time.

Use the simple formulation charts on page 56–57 to develop your formula drop by drop, this way if you do not like the end result, you can easily replicate your blend, but leaving out or adding ingredients as desired.

Once you have decided on your theme for your scent, using the Essential oils section from pages 38–45 as a guide, formulate your blend using scents applicable to your theme which complement each other. Write down each ingredient and the amounts you think you will use on the blank forms provided on page 56–57 or in a note book.

On pages 38–45 you will find that we have categorized the essential oils into top, middle and base notes. This is a guide only as oils vary from batch to batch depending on how they have been extracted, where they come from, and the type of species, therefore some may cross over the 'note' boundaries.

Find a good balance of top, middle and base notes. For instance, do not overpower a precious rose otto or jasmine with too many pungent spicy balsamic notes, let the 'celebrity' or special oils speak out for themselves, and surround them with oils that support and enhance them. This takes practise and skill and is also personal preference.

However, there are no hard and fast rules. Remember that you are creating your own scent, so if you think your choice of oils blend beautifully together, than your fragrance is a roaring success, as *you* are the customer.

You may wish to just take three oils – a top, middle and a base note – see how they blend together for your first formula, and then add in other ingredients, or change the amount of drops, in the second formula column. Start off with simple blends, with only small amounts of oil so that you do not make expensive mistakes. Once your confidence grows you can use more oils in your blends.

Using a pipette or bottle with a built-in dropper, drop the first essential oil from your written formula into a clean bottle. Make sure that the drop doesn't hit the sides of the glass bottle as the oil will cling to the sides for some time and you will not get the true amounts of oil in the bottom of your bottle.

You will need a different pipette for each essential oil. If you used the same pipette dipped into different oils they would be contaminated with different fragrances and would ruin your precious essential oils. You can purchase caps with built-in droppers for essential oil bottles which are perfect for this purpose

Make sure that all of your drops are roughly the same size – a drop from a pipette held sideways will create a much larger drop than one dropped from holding the pipette straight above the bottle.

## Approximate measures:

1ml = 20 drops
1tsp (5ml) = 100 drops
1 fluid oz (5 tsp) (25ml)

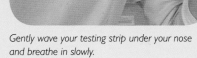

*Built-in dropper cap – cross each ingredient off your list as you blend to avoid mistakes.*

*Gently wave your testing strip under your nose and breathe in slowly.*

*Dip your testing strip in to your blend to soak up some of the fragrance for sampling.*

# Blend suggestions

## Aphrodisiac blend

The following formula is for the 'Having a Ball' recipe on page 97, which requires 1 teaspoon (5ml) of the final blend, which is very approximately 100 drops. Once you have made your blend, you will need to measure the amount using your teaspoon measure before adding to the recipe to make sure that it is the correct amount.

| Name of blend: Aphrodisiac | No. of drops/parts | No. of drops/parts | No. of drops/parts |
| --- | --- | --- | --- |
| Oil/fragrance | 1st formula | 2nd formula | 3rd formula |
| Bergamot | 35 | | |
| Jasmine | 20 | | |
| Rose fragrance | 20 | | |
| Black pepper | 10 | | |
| Ylang ylang | 3 | | |
| Frankincense | 12 | | |
| Total | 100 | | |

## Anti-fungal foot blend

This blend is used for 'Twinkle Toes' on page 123. We have used ingredients that are known to be deodorizing, antiseptic and anti-fungal to make your feet feel clean, refreshed and ready for dancing.

| Name of blend: Anti-fungal foot blend | No. of drops/parts | No. of drops/parts | No. of drops/parts |
| --- | --- | --- | --- |
| Oil/fragrance | 1st formula | 2nd formula | 3rd formula |
| Lemon | 15 | | |
| Lavender | 35 | | |
| Pine | 25 | | |
| Patchouli | 5 | | |
| Myrrh | 15 | | |
| Ginger | 5 | | |
| Total | 100 | | |

## 'Eau de Cologne' blend

There are many variations of this old-fashioned refreshing blend and we have given you some of the traditional ingredients used in Eau de Cologne. This is my version, but you might like to try making your own recipe in the 2nd formula column by tweaking the amounts of ingredients. For reference, the perfume was designed to have the odour of an Italian spring morning after the rain. Note: the recipe contains several oils that are phototoxic so do not expose the skin to ultra-violet light (sunlight or tanning bed) for 12 hours after using this recipe.

| Name of blend: Eau de Cologne | No. of drops/parts | No. of drops/parts | No. of drops/parts |
|---|---|---|---|
| Oil/fragrance | 1st formula | 2nd formula | 3rd formula |
| Bergamot | 32 | | |
| Petitgrain | 20 | | |
| Lemon | 30 | | |
| Neroli | 8 | | |
| Lavender | 4 | | |
| Orange | 36 | | |
| Rosemary | 2 | | |
| Total | 132 | | |

## Energy and concentration blend

This blend is used in the Herb Garden recipe on page 120. Once you have made your blend, measure the amount required for your recipe – the Herb Garden blend may make more than you will need. If you are using a small round bath bomb mould you can use up to 1½ teaspoons of the above blend in your recipe. You may like to adjust this recipe using the methods shown to create your very own bespoke blend.

| Name of blend: Herb Garden – Energy and concentration | No. of drops/parts | No. of drops/parts | No. of drops/parts |
|---|---|---|---|
| Oil/fragrance | 1st formula | 2nd formula | 3rd formula |
| Marjoram | 20 | | |
| Lavender | 70 | | |
| Rosemary | 10 | | |
| Cypress | 10 | | |
| Cedarwood | 20 | | |
| Total | 130 | | |

Once you have developed your new fragrance, leave it if possible for a few days as the oils will react and blend with each other over this time.

## Important note

Do not forget to label and date your blend and keep well away from children and pets. Store in a cool, dark place in a coloured glass bottle. After several days, dip your testing strip into your blend and sample the fragrance, waving it gently under your nostrils. Leave the testing strip for a few hours, come back and sample again. If you are happy with the fragrance, make a reference in your notes. Use the new blend to create your own bespoke bath bombs.

# Blank forms to photocopy

| Name of blend: | No. of drops/parts | No. of drops/parts | No. of drops/parts | No. of drops/parts |
|---|---|---|---|---|
| Oil/fragrance | 1st formula | 2nd formula | 3rd formula | 4th formula |
|  |  |  |  |  |
|  |  |  |  |  |
|  |  |  |  |  |
|  |  |  |  |  |
|  |  |  |  |  |
|  |  |  |  |  |
|  |  |  |  |  |

| Name of blend: | No. of drops/parts | No. of drops/parts | No. of drops/parts | No. of drops/parts |
|---|---|---|---|---|
| Oil/fragrance | 1st formula | 2nd formula | 3rd formula | 4th formula |
|  |  |  |  |  |
|  |  |  |  |  |
|  |  |  |  |  |
|  |  |  |  |  |
|  |  |  |  |  |
|  |  |  |  |  |

| Name of blend: | No. of drops/parts | No. of drops/parts | No. of drops/parts | No. of drops/parts |
|---|---|---|---|---|
| Oil/fragrance | 1st formula | 2nd formula | 3rd formula | 4th formula |
| | | | | |
| | | | | |
| | | | | |
| | | | | |
| | | | | |
| | | | | |
| | | | | |

| Name of blend: | No. of drops/parts | No. of drops/parts | No. of drops/parts | No. of drops/parts |
|---|---|---|---|---|
| Oil/fragrance | 1st formula | 2nd formula | 3rd formula | 4th formula |
| | | | | |
| | | | | |
| | | | | |
| | | | | |
| | | | | |
| | | | | |
| | | | | |

# Herbs, botanicals and additives

Aromatic oils and herbs from flowers, fruits, leaves, stems and roots have been used for thousands of years by all civilizations and tribes, using the plants that surrounded them to heal, worship, purify, beautify, to prevent disease and to bury the dead. Some civilizations, such as the Romans, brought their favourite herbs with them as they travelled, and plants that we still use today have been found in archaeological sites around the world.

Ancient art and manuscripts show that the civilizations of Egypt, China, Greece, Rome, India and Arabia used plant essences, herbs, botanicals, resins and aromatic oils medicinally, for worship, in cosmetics and in perfumes. They were considered more valuable than gold and the amount of precious oils and unguents you owned, and adorned your body with, were evidence of your wealth. Throughout history they have often been presented as expensive gifts, used in important religious ceremonies and banquets, in incense and sacrifice and to anoint brave travellers on their journeys.

Herbal medicines such as Chinese, Ayurvedic, Siddha and Tibb Unani medicine are important parts of cultures that have used nature's plants for thousands of years and, such is the belief in the power of the plant, are still practised and highly valued today. Other 'complementary therapies' that use nature's ingredients – flowers, herbs, oils and gums – such as aromatherapy, herbalism, flower remedies and homeopathy are now starting to play an important part in healthcare alongside modern medicine. It is important to note however that these are 'complementary' therapies and should not be used in place of conventional medical advice and treatment.

Some believe that within the plants that surround us there is the ability to heal and cure. Many forests are now being destroyed, where these possible cures for illness and disease are disappearing with the flora and fauna that used to grow beneath the forest canopies. It is therefore wise to try and purchase not only high-grade ingredients, but ones that have been ethically sourced from sustainable sources.

Organically grown ingredients are now more readily available to purchase; however, it is important to bear in mind that some ingredients that are produced by small local growers may have been grown organically, but they may not have the time, the money or local organisations to certify their products as 'organic'.

There are a myriad of ingredients available from all corners of the world providing endless possibilities for your bath bomb creations, which are only limited by your creativity. In creating your own fizzing sensation, you may decide to take inspiration from the shape of your mould, treat a particular ailment, or simply to create a relaxing fragrance with all of your favourite herbs and oils.

Will your bath bomb be for a man or a woman? Child or teenager? Sports enthusiast or couch potato? The following sections in this book will help you decide on some of the herbs, botanicals and other additives that you could use to create a tailor-made bath bomb for your family member, giving them a personal and special bathing experience. Do not be tempted to add every single ingredient that may apply to your ailment or theme, overloading it and making it too complicated. Sometimes just an uncoloured bath bomb, with one herb or essential oil can, in its simplicity, be just as pleasurable as one jam-packed full of lovely ingredients.

# Directory of common herbs, botanicals and other additives

## Bilberry
*Vaccinum myrtillus*
A dark purple-brown powder obtained from the bilberry fruit and leaf of a low-growing shrub which is mainly grown in the wild rather than cultivated. Also known as 'whinberries', they are related to blueberries and huckleberries. They are used in alternative medicine for the eyes and vision and for their effectiveness in maintaining general capillary health. Bilberries are known to be beneficial in the management of haemorrhoids, skin infections, burns, bruising, inflammation and rheumatism.

## Borage
*Borago officinalis*
Commonly known as 'starflower' due to its attractive blue star-shaped flowers which are often used in summer cocktails. A hairy-leafed plant with a cucumber scent originating from the Mediterranean. Borage was said to have been given to Roman Soldiers and the Crusaders for courage and is known as an aphrodisiac and helpful for depression. Borage oil has recently been found to be one of the richest sources of gamma-linolenic acid (GLA) which helps to repair the body. The oil is known to help inflammation, the hormonal system, PMS and menopause.

*Fresh borage flowers*

*Dried blue malva flowers*

## Blue malva flowers (mallow)
*Malva sylvestris*
A relative of the hollyhock and hibiscus, with pinky-mauve flowers and known as 'common mallow'. This native European plant grows on waste and rough ground, beside roads and railways and is thought to have been used medicinally by the Romans. Mallow contains mucilage, a glutinous sap which is a natural emollient known to soothe dry, rough skin.

## Burdock
*Arctium lappa*
Belonging to the thistle group, both the leaf and root of the plant are used. Their seed pods, with their natural hook and loop fasteners which enable the seed to be attached to animals, were apparently the inspiration for the modern day invention of fasteners made of nylon. The herb is well used as a blood purifier and to minimize boils, acne, eczema, ulcers, scaly and inflamed skin.

## Calendula (marigold) petals
*Calendula officinalis*
The orange-yellow petals of the marigold are a traditional remedy for minor skin problems such as cuts wounds and grazes and as well as providing beneficial skin-conditioning properties, these sunny yellow petals are also an attractive additive to your bath bomb. Calendula has long been used to help inflamed skin such as acne and sunburn and as a herbal remedy for athlete's foot, thrush and fungal conditions. Marigold has been used historically to help prevent infection from spreading and to speed up the process of cell regeneration.

## Chamomile powder or flowers

*Anthemis nobilis*

A strongly aromatic white flower with a yellow centre, very much like a daisy. Chamomile is an old favourite amongst garden herbs. The dried flowers are a pretty additive to floral or herbal bath bombs (the whole of the small flowers are yellow when dried) and the yellow powder will give your bomb a pale yellow-tan colour. Chamomile has been used historically for its sedative and relaxing properties and is known to soothe sensitive and irritated skin.

## Cinnamon

*Cinnamomum zeylanicum*

Cinnamon powder is a reddish-brown powder obtained from the bark of a small evergreen tree native to the Indian subcontinent. It is used to fight exhaustion and depression and is a known to help alleviate the aching muscles that come with colds and flu. Cinnamon is said to stimulate the circulation and benefit the aches and pains from rheumatism, arthritis and period pains. Use this spice sparingly – cinnamon is warming and stimulating but can irritate the skin if too much is used.

## Cocoa (chocolate) powder

*Theobrama cacao*

The non-fat components of the cacao bean which are known as cocoa solids. A dark brown powder, also known as chocolate powder, it is a high source of natural antioxidants known to protect and nourish the skin. This powder has a deliciously sweet chocolate smell and imparts a pale brown colour when mixed into your bath bomb mixture – surely a must for all the chocolate lovers. This is a great additive when combined with moisturizing cocoa butter, the fatty part of the cacao bean, which is separated from the solids at the beginning of the extraction process.

## Comfrey

*Symphytum officinale*

A hairy-leafed plant with light purple, cream or pink flowers related to borage and forget-me-nots. Both the leaf and the roots are used in herbal medicine and it is widely used as an organic fertilizer. Famously known as 'knitbone' for its ability to 'knit' or heal the flesh, comfrey contains a natural compound called allantoin which promotes cell healing and the growth of healthy tissue and soothes, protects and softens up the skin. Comfrey also contains mucilage, a gooey polymer that acts as a membrane thickener (also found in aloe vera, cactus and marshmallow) which forms a soothing film over mucus membrane thereby relieving pain and inflammation. Comfrey is widely used in herbalism today for healing broken bones, sprains, cuts, wounds, skin irritation, bruises and for the easing of pain, inflammation, haemorrhoids and gout.

## Cornstarch/cornflour (or maize starch)

*Zea mays*

A creamy-white powdery substance made from maize (corn) which is soft and gentle and often used as an alternative to talc in baby products. You can add cornstarch (cornflour) to bath bombs, which can even the texture and absorb the liquid, giving a smooth finish and may also help your bomb to bob along on the surface of the water. Try adding ¼ cup (40g/1½oz) cornstarch (cornflour) to your basic recipe with your other dry ingredients.

*Cinnamon sticks and powder*

*Fresh comfrey*

## Cranberry powder

*Vaccinium macrocarpon*

Cranberries are a low-growing, woody plant widely grown in the USA and Canada. Cranberries are packed with vitamins and are high in antioxidants and are known to have powerful anti-inflammatory properties.

## Epsom salts

*Magnesium sulphate*

White, sparkly crystals that look similar to sea salt, Epsom salts were named after an English town where the salt was produced by boiling down the local mineral-rich water. It is reported that soaking in an Epsom salt bath can increase your magnesium levels. This may have benefits that include easing muscle pain, relieving stress and insomnia and reducing the severity of diabetes. Epsom salts are also known to have wonderful detoxification properties helping the body to flush out toxins, taking the sting out of insect bites, drawing out splinters, promoting circulation, and the deep cleansing of the skin and pores. Try using ¼ cup (70g/2½oz) of Epsom salt to your basic recipe with your other dry ingredients.

## Flower remedies

Developed in the 1930s by Dr Edward Bach, a doctor, who, dissatisfied with orthodox medicine and inspired by homeopathy, created flower-based remedies for 38 negative states of mind. He believed that certain plants infused in spring water and left in the sun to impart their properties, transmitted their 'energies' to the user. Using similar methods, the more recently created Australian Bush Remedies, designed by naturopath Ian White from his understanding of Australia's natural bush plants, are said to dissolve subconscious negative beliefs and restore balance to the mind, body and spirit.

## Ginger powder

*Zingiber officinale*

Widely used in Chinese medicine Ginger is known to be stimulating and warming. Dried ginger is said to help colds, stomach pain, nausea, digestion, cough, rheumatism, arthritis, muscle ache and inflammation. It is known to be an anti-oxidant with aphrodisiac properties.

## Ginkgo biloba

*Ginkgo biloba*

Large trees with bright yellow leaves known in China as 'silver fruit' thought to have been cultivated in China for over 1,500 years. Known to improve memory and concentration, circulation, energy levels and as a powerful antioxidant and anti-inflammatory.

Epsom salts

Ginkgo biloba leaves

Green tea powder

## Ginseng

*Panax ginseng*

Meaning 'the wonder of the world' or 'all-heal', originating from Asia. Used in Chinese herbalism for thousands of years it is used for focusing the mind, fatigue, the immune system, stress, circulation and inflammation, as an aphrodisiac and a general healthy tonic for conditioning and rejuvenating the skin.

## Green tea

*Camellia sinensis*

Green tea has been used in China, Japan, India and Thailand for digestion, lowering blood sugar and for healing wounds for centuries. It is known to be a powerful antioxidant containing a wide variety of vitamins and minerals which help to protect the skin. It is also known to have skin rejuvenating and healing properties and has been used to help athlete's foot, bedsores and skin disease.

## Goat's milk powder

*Caprae lac*

Moisturizing and nourishing and rich in vitamins A, B12, D, K and contains iodine, potassium, magnesium and selenium. Goat's milk is said to be a wonderful emollient helping to sooth conditions such as eczema and psoriasis.

## Hops

*Humulus lupulus*

A well-known native British plant used as an additive in beer making. Hops are valuable in aiding sleep and are a traditional cure for insomnia. They are known to possess sedative properties helping to ease nervous complaints, relax muscles, improve the appetite and soften the skin.

## Jasmine flowers

*Jasmine officinale*

Derived from the Persian name 'Yasmin' meaning 'gift from God', jasmine flowers are the small white flowers that adorn pretty-leaved, hardy climbers which are extensively cultivated for their exquisite scent in Grasse, France, for the perfume market (see page 48). Known as an anti-depressant, and used to help lack of energy, listlessness, digestion, IBS and as an aphrodisiac.

## Kelp powder

*Laminaria digitata*

Kelp are large nutrient-rich sea plants (algae), commonly referred to as 'seaweed'. Abundant in amino acids, iodine and vitamins, Kelp is used to tone, detox, moisturize and revitalize the skin and boost immunity. This powdered marine plant will leave browny-green flecks of seaweed throughout your bomb making it a great additive to spa- or ocean-themed bath bombs. Kelp will, however, generally smell strongly of seaweed so you will need to make allowances when fragrancing your product. Do not add too much to your bath bomb as it will smell very strongly.

Goat's milk powder          Kelp powder

## Lavender

*Lavandula angustifolia*

Widely grown commercially for use in the perfumery industry after the flowers are distilled, lavender has also been used for centuries in pot pourri, to scent linen, to fragrance the home and as a moth deterrent. The essential oil has many benefits which are listed in the essential oil section on page 41 and lavender buds will make an attractive and relaxing additive to your bath bombs. You may even decide not to use your bath bomb in the bath, and instead place it in an organza bag or wrap in a piece of muslin to scent your linen drawer.

## Lemon peel powder

*Citrus medica limonum*

Lemon peel powder can give a good natural colouring to your bath bombs and enhance any citrus oils used to fragrance your recipe. Rich in vitamin C, lemon is used in alternative medicine to help the immune system, colds, infection and influenza, to detoxify, assist lymphatic drainage, digestion and as a skin tonic.

## Lemon balm

*Melissa officinalis*

Heart-shaped, deliciously lemon-scented leaves that can be used as a substitute for lemon in cooking. Balm was an ingredient in Carmelite water or 'Eau de Carmes', a seventeenth-century perfumed toilet water created by Carmelite monks which was also taken internally for nervous headaches and neuralgia. Known to be effective for the nervous system, depression, memory, headache, insomnia, herpes, colds and fevers, and insect bites.

## Linden

*Tilia vulgaris*

A tree attaining a height of up to 130ft (40m) and known as the 'lime tree', not to be confused with tropical lime fruit trees. The tree produces fragrant flowers, which have been used for hundreds of years for nervous conditions, anxiety, nervous headaches, insomnia, high blood pressure and stress. It is also used to ease colds and fevers and to treat dry skin.

## Nettle

*Urtica dioica*

A herbaceous, flowering plant with stinging hairs giving it the name 'stinging nettle'. The leaves are high in nutrients such as A, C, D, iron, potassium, manganese, calcium and nitrogen and once cooked, or crushed, the chemicals in the leaves that cause the sting will be destroyed. Nettle has a long history and a multitude of uses. It is recorded that Roman soldiers rubbed nettle leaf on their skin to treat cold aching limbs and brought the seeds of the plant with them when they travelled as the plant was so useful to them.

In the past, fibres of the plant were used to make sails, sacks and linen and to produce a permanent green dye. Similar to mallow and comfrey, nettle contains the emollient 'mucilage', minerals, formic acid, beta-carotene, phosphates, iron and is rich in vitamins A, C, D and B complex.

Nettle is used as an astringent and a stimulating tonic, particularly for the hair. As a diuretic it is said to stimulate the kidneys and bladder and detoxify the body. It is known to help the symptoms of gout and arthritis and to stimulate the immune system.

*Lemon balm*

*Dried nettle leaves*

## Rose petals (dog rose)

*Rosa canina*

Rose petals are a most attractive additive to your bath bombs and you will only need a pinch as a little goes a long way. For the benefits and properties of rose see page 44 in the essential oils section.

## Sea salt and Dead Sea salt

*Maris sal*

Mineral-rich sea salt crystals from the ocean have been used for centuries for their therapeutic and healing properties, leaving the skin clean, soft and detoxified. The Dead Sea, once part of the ocean, is now a lake with extremely high levels of salt and minerals containing more than eight times the amount of salt as other oceans. The salinity of the water is so high that fish and plant life are unable to live in the mineral-rich water, hence the name the 'Dead Sea'. Situated between Israel and Jordan, it is the lowest natural place on earth.

The water is rich in magnesium, potassium, calcium chlorides and contains high concentrations of bromides which are believed to be beneficial for the treatment of psoriasis, eczema, muscular pain, arthritis and rheumatism. These salts are used to relieve tension, insomnia and promote relaxation.

For thousands of years kings and queens have travelled far and wide to bathe in the Dead Sea. The salt is now easily obtained from pharmacies and health food shops, making it easy to create your own mineral-rich sea in your own bathroom.

## Wheatgrass powder

*Triticum vulgare*

A vivid green powder obtained from the dried young sprouting leaves of wheatgrass. It is packed full of all vitamins, minerals and enzymes containing a high proportion of chlorophyll, hence the colour, which is known to be beneficial for the immune system. It is reported to remove toxins from the body, help acne and scars and to restore damaged skin tissue.

## Whey powder

Powdered whey is a cream-coloured fine powder which is made by dehydrating the liquid left after straining curdled milk. Rich in valuable amino acids, minerals, vitamins and lactic acid which regulates the pH of the skin, it is known to be effective for smoothing dry scaly skin, for stimulating and deep cleansing the skin cells and for soothing eczema, psoriasis and sunburn. Cleopatra was famous for her beautiful skin which was reputedly obtained by frequently bathing in a luxurious milky bath.

*Basic ingredients*

*Dried rose petals*

*Sea salt*

*Wheatgrass powder*

*Whey powder*

# Colour

You can, of course, leave your bath bombs white and uncoloured. White represents cleanliness, peace and purity and contains a little of every colour in the visible light spectrum. However, without our knowing, colour can play an important role in our lives and can affect our moods and sense of wellbeing. The ancient Egyptians and the Chinese are said to have used colour as healing 'cures' and although lost for a long time, 'colour therapy' is now being applied by businesses, hospitals, prisons and product ranges as people are becoming aware again of the importance of colour in our lives.

Some colours can relax and calm, while others can stimulate and revive. Visualizing colour can also affect our sense of smell. Try an experiment – make a batch of uncoloured bath bombs fragranced with lemongrass. Colour half with yellow and leave the other half white. Ask your friends and family to try and guess which has the strongest smell and you will probably find that the majority of people will perceive the coloured bath bomb to have the strongest scent.

It is widely known that colour can also influence our moods. A vase of vibrant red flowers in the middle of a dining table will promote lively conversation, energy and a successful dinner party. Pale blue flowers would promote a relaxing, calm atmosphere.

Once you have chosen the theme and scent of your bath bomb you can finally choose the colour. Choose a colour that will naturally complement and enhance your bath bomb, for instance a herbaceous-smelling bath bomb would make sense if coloured green, and an ocean-scented bath bomb would be enhanced by shades of blue or turquoise.

*It is not just fragrance that can affect our moods, the colour you choose for your bath bombs is important too.*

# Colour associations

Different colours are believed to be associated with various parts of the body, helping to ease problems in certain areas. It is said that you are often subconsciously drawn to a particular colour that relates to a problem that you may be experiencing.

**Red:** Power, passion, love, excitement, circulation, adrenalin, reviving, energising. Known to help muscle aches, lethargy and tiredness.

**Blue:** Calming, restful, peaceful, relaxing. Known to help the throat, upper arms and lungs.

**Orange:** Gentle strength, optimism, creativity, promotes change. Known to help the lower back, kidneys, abdomen, bronchitis.

**Turquoise:** Affairs of the heart, panic, shock, restorative. Known to help areas of the throat and chest.

**Yellow:** Alertness, depression, laughter, joy, fun, cheerful, revitalizing. Known to help the stomach, liver, digestive system, detoxification, depression.

**Purple:** Protection and leadership, spiritual awareness, concentration, rejuvenation. Known to help the head, scalp and immune system.

**Green:** Harmonizing, shock, fatigue, healing, balance, stamina. Known to help the heart, chest and lungs.

**Pink:** The colour pink contains red and will have the same properties of red but with a more gentle effect, such as love, warmth, nurture and tranquillity.

# Colouring bath bombs

After adding the colour to your dry bath bomb mixture, the colour of your mixture will look pale. Do NOT be tempted to add more colour. When you add your oils and water the colour will darken and intensify. Upon drying, your bath bomb will turn pale but the colour will intensify again when plunged into a bath. For this reason, the finished products will not be vibrantly coloured, but delicate pastel shades. If your finished bath bomb is too coloured and intense, you may end up staining your bath. There are various ways to colour your bath bombs: liquid colour, coloured pigments, natural herbs or spices.

## Liquid colours or bath bomb dyes

The easiest cosmetic colours for use in bath bombs are liquid colours. For the recipes in this book you will need cosmetic grade liquid blue, liquid red, liquid yellow and liquid green. These colours can be blended together to create different shades (see the colour blending chart on page 71). You will be able to obtain these colours from soap or bath-bomb-making suppliers (see page 144). You can also use liquid food colouring from your kitchen cupboard; however, these are not always reliable and can fade pretty quickly. We recommend using cosmetic grade colours for the best results.

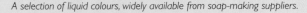

*Beware of adding too much colour as you may risk staining your bath.*

*A selection of liquid colours, widely available from soap-making suppliers.*

## Pigments

Pigments are powdered colours made up of small particles which are dispersed and suspended in your bath water. They are named ultramarines, oxides and chromium greens. These powdered substances were originally mined from earth and rocks; however, these naturally mined mineral pigments also contained high levels of toxic and unsafe minerals. These days, although chemically the same, they are reproduced so that the pigments are safe and non-toxic for use in the cosmetics industry.

These powdered colour pigments are very strong and dense, a tiny amount will go a very long way. So beware, if too much is used, you can end up colouring your bath, yourself and your towels, so they are really best left to the experienced bath bomb maker. Pigments, however, will not fade as quickly as the liquid colours. We would recommend using, at the very maximum, ¼ teaspoon of the following pigments in your basic recipe (see page 24).

**Ultramarines**
Ultramarine Light Blue
Ultramarine Pink
Ultramarine Violet
(You will also find 'Ultramarine Blue' available for sale as opposed to the Ultramarine 'Light Blue', but this is best avoided as it can smell like bad eggs with certain bath bomb recipe combinations, so purchase a 'light blue' or odour-free blue)

**Oxides**
Iron Oxide
Chromium Green Oxide (Green Chrome Oxide)
Hydrated Chromium Oxide (Hydrated Green Chrome Oxide) (a green/blue)
Black Iron Oxide
Yellow Oxide

*Pigments, from top, clockwise:*
*Chromium Green Oxide, Ultramarine Violet,*
*Ultramarine Blue and Ultramarine Pink.*

## Natural colours derived from plants

Powdered forms of herbs, spices, flowers and other natural materials can be used to colour and enhance your bath bombs. It is important to note however that natural ingredients are just that – 'natural ingredients', and as such they can fade pretty quickly, some more than others, depending on their chemical make-up. It is therefore even more important that bath bombs are not left next to a window with sunlight streaming in. Fragrances and colour can be destroyed by sunlight in as little as half an hour.

The list of natural ingredients are endless; below are a few suggestions of the ingredients that you can use in your recipes. We would recommend using up to 1 tablespoon of powdered herbs in your basic recipe (see page 24).

cayenne powder

paprika powder

comfrey powder

rosemary powder

lavender powder

wheatgrass powder

orange peel powder

sage powder

coffee powder

kelp (seaweed)

turmeric powder

cinnamon powder

spirulina powder

goat's milk powder

rose powder

honey powder

cranberry powder

lemon peel powder

chocolate powder

green tea powder

chamomile powder

*Natural colour, from top, clockwise: wheatgrass powder, comfrey powder and goat's milk powder.*

# Cosmetic glitters

There are many different coloured cosmetic glitters available from ingredient suppliers which can add colour and sparkle to your bath bombs. Only cosmetic grade glitters should be used, not hobby craft glitters, as they are not suitable for bath products.

There is a whole rainbow of cosmetic glitter colours available, from blues, greens, pinks and lavenders to silver, gold bronze and crystalline (which are like a thousand little crystals floating in your water). The size of the glitter particles can vary from different suppliers and larger glitter 'shapes' are also available as hearts, stars and strands.

A little always goes a long way, so we recommend using approximately ½ to 1 teaspoon of glitter depending on the size of the glitter particle.

*A small selection of the many glitters available from ingredient suppliers.*

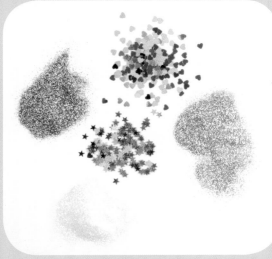

# Caution

- If you are using glitters in the bath make sure that you do not submerge your whole head under the water as glitter should be kept away from the eyes.

- If you are using oils or butters in your bath bomb with coloured pigments, you may find that the pigments will stick to the oil leaving a coloured ring around your bath. Avoid using excess colour or herbs in your bath fizz as they could leave a stain.

- Colours and their strength may vary from supplier to supplier, so if you are using a colour for the first time, use it sparingly until you get used to the intensity and behaviour of your colour.

- The 'raw' colours are intense and only a little is needed. It would be wise to cover up your clothing and work surfaces when handling colour and wash any areas of contact straight away to avoid staining.

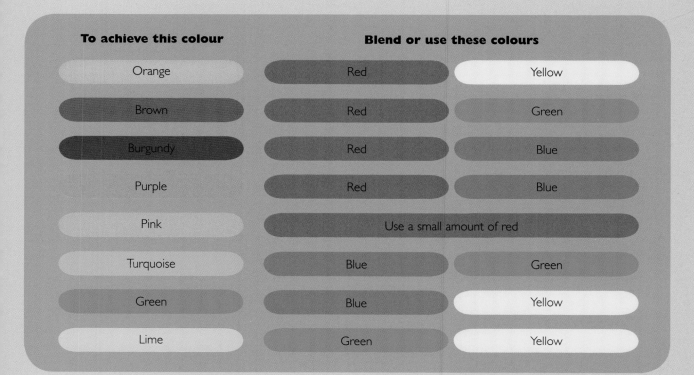

| To achieve this colour | Blend or use these colours | |
| --- | --- | --- |
| Orange | Red | Yellow |
| Brown | Red | Green |
| Burgundy | Red | Blue |
| Purple | Red | Blue |
| Pink | Use a small amount of red | |
| Turquoise | Blue | Green |
| Green | Blue | Yellow |
| Lime | Green | Yellow |

# Oils and butters

From ancient Egyptian, Roman and Greek literature, history shows us that oils extracted from plants, known as vegetable oils, have been an important part of history for thousands of years. Nature has given us an abundance of seeds, nuts and kernels contained in the fruits of plants, providing numerous oils and butters from all areas of the world such as African shea butter, Asian mango butter, Chinese rice bran oil, American macadamia nut oil and Mediterranean olive oil. Extremely luxurious, moisturizing and rich in nutrients, on the next few pages we have selected just a few oils for you to try in your bath bomb recipes to give your skin a treat.

As you will see, vegetable oils and butters can be used in your bath bombs to nourish, moisturize, soothe and revitalize dry, tired or lifeless skin. They also have known therapeutic benefits which are used for skin conditions such as eczema and psoriasis, aching muscles or to help the appearance of scars and wrinkles. They vary widely in thickness, colour and aroma: the lighter, more easily absorbed oils are suitable for normal to oily skins, whilst the thicker, heavier oils and butters are beneficial to those with dry or mature skin.

## What is a butter?

A 'butter' is a naturally sourced, hard vegetable fat obtained from the kernels, or nuts, of plants which are solid at room temperature. High in healthy, essential fatty acids, vitamins and minerals, many are widely used in cooking and are a luxurious ingredient in the cosmetics and body care industries. The term 'butter' is slightly misleading as they do not have anything to do with dairy products that are normally associated with the word 'butter'. To use butters in your bath bombs, you will need to gently heat them until they are liquid – you will find full instructions on how to melt your oils on page 31.

# What are vegetable oils?

Vegetable oils are liquid at room temperature and are obtained by traditionally crushing, pressing and usually refining the seeds and nuts of plants. These essential parts of the plant's system contain high levels of different fatty acids, vitamins and minerals with known antioxidant, anti-inflammatory and moisturizing properties.

The versatility of vegetable oils are legendary and have a multitude of uses. Apart from their obvious use in the food industry, many oils are widely used to make soaps, skin care, cosmetics and candles. Vegetable oils have also been used historically to make paint and to treat wood and are now widely used as lubricants, electrical insulators and in the production of biodiesel.

Liquid oils and butters are a wonderful addition to your bath bombs to nourish, pamper and protect your skin. The lighter oils such as grapeseed, sweet almond and apricot are the most easily dispersed oils in your bath water and will make cleaning your bath slightly easier than the other oils; however, small amounts of other heavier oils or butters can provide excellent emollient and moisturizing properties, although they will leave your bath oily.

# Caution when using oils

The heavier oils will not be as evenly distributed throughout your bath water as the lighter oils and may leave your bath greasy. We would not recommend using oils in bath bombs that are to be used by the elderly, children, or people who have difficulty in climbing out of the bath, as the oils can make the bath slippery. Care should always be taken by anyone climbing out of a bath with an oily residue.

Do not expect oils to smell of the original fruit or plant such as mango butter or raspberry oil, as most butters do not usually have the familiar scent of the actual fruit. However, each oil will still have its unique aroma which you will need to make allowances for when scenting your bombs as they may change the overall fragrance of your bath bomb.

*Basic ingredients*

# Directory of common oils and butters

## Apricot kernel oil
*Prunus armeniaca*
Pressed from the kernel of the apricot fruit this light oil, pale in colour, is readily absorbed into the skin and is similar to sweet almond or peach oil. It is high in essential fatty acids, linoleic and oleic acids, and is said to be beneficial and nourishing to sensitive, dehydrated and mature skin. It is used in skincare for treating fine lines, delicate and sensitive areas. An emollient, containing Vitamin A, helping to diminish the appearance of stretch marks and increase the skin's elasticity.

## Argan oil
*Argania spinosa*
The kernels of the ancient Argan tree, which is endemic to the dry, desert conditions of Morocco and North Africa, are hand-pressed to produce this oil. Similar in properties to olive oil, Argan oil contains fatty acids and high levels of vitamin E, a powerful antioxidant. The oil has been traditionally used by the Berber people for centuries to nourish and protect the skin and to promote the skin's elasticity, thereby helping to reduce the appearance scars and wrinkles.

## Avocado oil
*Persea gratissima*
Avocado oil is obtained by pressing the flesh of the fruit as opposed to the seeds, the oil is a dark green colour containing chlorophyll. It is easily absorbed into the skin and is widely used for sun-damaged or dehydrated skin, eczema and psoriasis. It has wonderfully emollient properties making it ideal for rejuvenating and softening mature skin. Avocado oil is rich in vitamins A, B1, B2, D and vitamin E as well as lecithin and potassium.

## Castor oil
*Ricinus communis*
Obtained from the castor bean, castor oil acts as a humecant, drawing moisture to the skin and providing a protective barrier against the environment. Castor oil is also used for sunburn, skin irritation, burns and cuts and is reputed to ease various ailments such as inflammation and muscle pains.

*Avocado oil*

## Cocoa butter

*Theobroma cacao*

Cocoa butter is the fatty component of chocolate, which is produced from the cacao bean. Cocoa solids (chocolate powder) and cocoa butter are separated at the early stages of production for use in different manufacturing processes; they are also brought together again and used in the production of chocolate. Cocoa butter on its own is used in the making of white chocolate without the cocoa solids (chocolate powder). The name *Theobroma* means 'food of the gods' and anyone who is a chocoholic will understand why.

It is possible to purchase unrefined cocoa butter which has a dark creamy colour with a fantastic chocolaty aroma – you will have to use all of your willpower not to eat it! In most places, however, you will find the white, refined, cocoa butter that has no smell, which is useful if you wish to have all of the nutrients that cocoa butter provides but do not wish to have a chocolate smell to your products.

Cocoa butter is said to provide a protective barrier to retain the moisture in your skin. As a source of natural antioxidants it is known to help dry skin and wrinkles and is often used in suntan lotions, and in skincare to help stretch marks and scars.

## Evening primrose oil

*Oenothera biennis*

A pale yellow oil produced from the seeds of the evening primrose flower. High in gamma-linolenic acid (GLA or omega 6) it is used to help ease eczema, psoriasis and dry skin. Evening primrose oil is easily absorbed by the skin and used in skin preparations to prevent premature ageing.

## Grapeseed oil

*Vitis vinifera seed*

A bi-product of the wine-making industry, grapeseed oil is made from the seeds of grapes. It is easily absorbed into the skin and finer than sweet almond, making it an excellent additional oil for bath bombs as it will leave the least amount of oil on your skin and in the bath. Used in the cosmetics industry to support cell membranes, reduce the appearance of stretch marks and to help repair damaged skin tissue.

## Hazelnut oil

*Corylus americana nut*

Grown in Northern Europe with long yellow catkins which appear in the spring, the oil is pressed from the hazelnuts. A vitamin-rich oil with excellent emollient properties, containing high levels of thiamine (vitamin B1) and vitamin B6. Hazelnut oil has long been used for the treatment of dry, damaged skin and is reported to be helpful in filtering the rays of the sun and thus is used in many suncare products.

*Basic ingredients*

Cocoa butter

Evening primrose

Grapeseed oil

## Hempseed oil
*Cannabis sativa*
Extracted from the seeds of the hemp plant which is high in important unsaturated fatty acids including palmitoleic, oleic, linoleic and GLA. Hempseed oil is widely used in cosmetics due to the unique balance of its essential fatty acids (EFAs) which complements the proportions of EFAs required by the human body. Hempseed oil is reported to help reduce inflammation and to ease the symptoms of eczema and psoriasis.

## Jojoba oil
*Simmondsia chinensis*
A native shrub from the deserts of Arizona, California and Mexico, jojoba oil is actually a liquid wax obtained from the seeds of the plant. Jojoba oil is similar to our own skin's sebum, the protective oily substance secreted from our sebaceous glands making it readily absorbed by the skin. It is often used in the cosmetics industry as a fragrance carrier oil and as a moisturizer in skincare products. Rich in proteins and minerals, jojoba is used to help soothe eczema, psoriasis, dry and sensitive skin.

## Macadamia nut oil
*Macadamia ternifolia*
The oil is produced from the nuts of a Native American tree and contains high levels of palmitoleic acid which is a substance similar to the skin's sebum – the oily substance secreted by the sebaceous glands produced to protect the skin from becoming dry and from the growth of micro-organisms. Production of the skin's sebum reduces with time, resulting in drier skin as we age; macadamia nut oil is known to help rejuvenate mature, dry and ageing skin and to aid stretch marks and burns.

## Mango butter
*Mangifera indica*
Grown mainly in Burma, Southern Asia and Northern India (*indica* meaning from India), mango butter is obtained from the fruit kernels of the tropical mango or Mangifera tree. Mango butter is used for many applications including treating dry, sunburned skin and in aiding protection from the sun, for wounds and rough skin, scars and wrinkles, eczema, psoriasis and dermatitis.

*Jojoba oil*

*Mango butter*

## Monoi de Tahiti

*Cocos nucifera – Gardenia tahitensis*

The French Polynesians produce their Monoi de Tahiti by the process of 'enfleurage' (see page 36) with exotic petals from their native 'Tiare' flowers being gently macerated in refined coconut oil (*Cocos nucifera*). This ancient method produces an exquisite, sweet, floral aroma making it a delightfully fragrant and moisturizing additive to your bath bombs. Due to many inferior copies of this oil being sold, Monoi de Tahiti is now a registered 'Appellation d'Origine', which carries a logo assuring the authenticity and quality of this delightful oil.

## Olive oil

*Olea europaea*

Grown mainly in the Mediterranean, olive oil is a green to golden brown colour depending on the grade or quality. The oil is traditionally obtained by grinding sun-ripened olives to a pulp, the material is then pressed to extract the oil. Homer, the ancient Greek poet, called olive oil 'liquid gold' as the ancient Greeks rubbed the oil infused with flowers and grasses into their bodies to promote strength and youth. Olive oil is a complex compound made of fatty acids, high in oleic acid, vitamin A, vitamin E (a natural antioxidant), vitamin K and other important vitamins and minerals. The properties of olive oil are said to be helpful for burns, inflammation, arthritis, wounds and dry skin.

## Pumpkin seed oil

*Cucurbita pepo*

This oil is made by pressing the roasted, hulled pumpkin seeds and is usually a very dark green, sometimes referred to as 'green gold'. It is an extremely nutritious and nourishing oil, containing many important active constituents. High in essential fatty acids, omega 3, omega 6 and omega 9, vitamins A, C, E and zinc, pumpkin seed oil is rich in Vitamin E, a powerful antioxidant which can help diminish the appearance of stretch marks and wrinkles and can help ease the effects of psoriasis.

## Raspberry seed oil

*Rubus idaeus*

Extracted from the seeds of the raspberry fruit. Raspberry seed oil is reputed to be an excellent antioxidant, high in essential fatty acids and vitamin E, which is known to play an important role in the repair of skin damage. Its superior anti-inflammatory properties are high on the scale compared with other oils and it is particularly useful in facial skincare as an emollient and helping to soothe the symptoms of eczema, rashes and overheated, irritated skin. Raspberry seed oil has been reputedly shown to act as a UV filter and is a valuable ingredient in sun-blocks and sun-screens.

*Monoi de Tahiti*

*Pumpkin seed oil*

*Raspberry seed oil*

*Basic ingredients*

## Rice bran oil

*Oryza sativa*

Extracted from the germ and inner husk of rice, rice bran oil is a mild and softening oil that has long been used in Japan to protect and moisturize mature or sensitive skin. High in essential fatty acids and vitamin E it provides excellent anti-oxidant properties. Rice bran oil is also rich in oleic and linoleic acid, and is known to help inflammation, dry and ageing skin.

## Rosehip oil

*Rosa canina* or *Rosa moschata*

Obtained from the seeds of rosehips, which are also used in jams, jellies, syrups and teas because of their high vitamin E content. Uniquely for vegetable oils, rosehip oil also contains retinol (vitamin A) in addition to other essential fatty acids, which is said to help delay the effects of skin ageing. Rosehip oil is widely used in skincare products for its regenerating properties and is known to help dry, damaged, scarred skin, pigmentation and stretch marks. The oil is easily absorbed into the skin and is useful for all skin types.

## Shea butter

*Butyrospermum parkii*

A rich, creamy natural fat that is obtained by boiling, drying and roasting the nuts of the fruit of the African Karite tree. A highly emollient butter with a low natural sun protection, although this should not be relied on for sunbathing. Shea butter is solid at room temperature, but melts on contact with the skin. It is used for its effectiveness at helping to lessen the appearance of many skin blemishes including scars, stretch marks, burns, rashes and eczema. A most versatile oil, shea butter is rich in nutrients and highly prized for its anti-ageing and moisturizing properties.

The most luxurious shea butter is 'unrefined' which retains all of its nutrients in abundance. The only treatment the product has usually received is filtration, for use in the cosmetic industry. Unrefined shea butter is very rich and creamy in texture and colour with a strong, nutty flavour. This scent is relatively pungent however, so if you wish to purchase a less odorous shea butter you are best to go for the whiter, 'refined' version.

## Strawberry seed oil

*Fragaria vesca* (or *Fragaria ananassa*)

Containing some of the most powerful sources of antioxidants found in nature, this luxurious oil is high in gamma tocopherol and is a valuable source of essential fatty acids such as linoleic, alpha-linoleic and oleic acid, making it a wonderful anti-ageing ingredient. Highly emollient, with a light texture and subtle aroma, this oil is effective in helping dry and damaged skin.

*Rosehips*

*Shea butter*

## Sweet almond oil

*Prunus dulcis*

Pressed from the kernels of the sweet almond fruit and prized since ancient times. The oil is very widely used as a carrier oil as it is non-greasy and easily absorbed by the skin. Sweet almond oil contains vitamins A, B1, B2, B6 and E. A wonderful emollient used to nourish, protect and condition the skin, to calm skin irritation and to soften dry skin.

## Vitamin E

*Tocopherol*

Fat-soluble antioxidants, which are found in a variety of fruit and vegetables and are known to protect against cell-damaging free radicals produced by pollution, fried food, stress, sunbathing and infection. It is claimed that vitamin E is also effective in helping to reduce the appearance of stretch marks, age spots, scars, dry, ageing skin and to keep the skin looking younger by reducing the appearance of lines and wrinkles. Vitamin E is a thick, viscous liquid that can be purchased in capsules from your local drug store or chemist. Simply open the capsule and add the liquid at the same time as the other ingredients in your bath bomb.

## Wheatgerm oil

*Triticum vulgare germ*

An emollient oil expressed from the germ of the wheat kernel. Wheatgerm oil is very high in essential fatty acids, vitamin E, A, D and linoleic acid (omega 6). The oil is used for dry, cracked skin and for its antioxidant properties, which help to detoxify and protect the skin from environmental pollutants. A nourishing and skin-conditioning oil, it is helpful in assisting with the repair of sun-damaged, dehydrated and sensitive skin.

*Sweet almond tree*

*Wheatgerm oil*

# Recipes

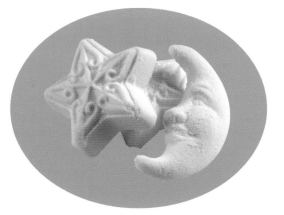

Calming chamomile and relaxing lavender blend perfectly to make this soothing recipe that will help to promote a good night's sleep and happy dreams.

# Milky Whey

*See pages 24–26 for basic bath bomb recipe instructions*

## Ingredients

300g (11oz or 1 cup) granulated citric acid

600g (1lb 5oz or 2 cups) bicarbonate of soda (baking soda)

2 tablespoons whey powder

2 tablespoons goat's milk powder

¼ teaspoon Roman chamomile essential oil

½ teaspoon lavender essential oil

## Moulds

Star and moon mould

## Quantity

This recipe will make approximately 13 stars and 3 moons

### *Other ideas*

**Other mould suggestions:**

*half round sphere or any star shapes*

**Other fragrance ideas:**

*mandarin or sweet orange essential oil*

Used for centuries in the traditional ritual of the Japanese tea ceremony, green tea is also known to be a wonderful antioxidant containing many vitamins and minerals.

# Green Tea

*See pages 24–26 for basic bath bomb recipe instructions*

## Ingredients

300g (11oz or 1 cup) granulated citric acid
600g (1lb 5oz or 2 cups) bicarbonate of soda (baking soda)
1 teaspoon green tea fragrance oil
1 teaspoon liquid green colour (or ¼ teaspoon
    chromium green oxide powder)
1 tablespoon green tea powder

## Moulds

Teapot-shaped chocolate making mould

## Quantity

This recipe makes 6 teapots

**Caution**
If using powdered colour, do not exceed the stated amount to avoid colouring your bath.

Add a little sparkle to your water with these refreshing and uplifting bath bombs. Pop one of these in the bath, close your eyes and imagine yourself skiing off-piste in fresh powder snow.

*See pages 24–26 for basic bath bomb recipe instructions*

## Ingredients

300g (11oz or 1 cup) granulated citric acid
600g (1lb 5oz or 2 cups) bicarbonate of soda (baking soda)
1 teaspoon snow fragrance oil
½–1 teaspoon cosmetic grade glitter

## Moulds

Pine tree, snowballs and stars

## Quantity

This recipe makes 4 stars, 4 snowballs and 1 tree

### *Other ideas*

**Other mould suggestions:**
*any rounds or spheres*

**Other fragrance ideas:**
*any fresh, uplifting fragrance with a top, or green note, such as pine essential oil, neroli, bergamot or citrus oils*

A great pick-me-up after a hard game of tennis or sports. The tangy citrus oils are known to give a boost of energy and also deodorize, whilst juniper stimulates the circulation.

# Game, Set and Match

*See pages 24–26 for basic bath bomb recipe instructions*

## Quantity
This recipe makes 8 tennis balls

## Ingredients
300g (11oz or 1 cup) granulated citric acid
600g (1lb 5oz or 2 cups) bicarbonate of soda (baking soda)
1 teaspoon wheatgrass powder (optional or could use comfrey herb)
¼ teaspoon lime essential oil
¼ teaspoon grapefruit essential oil
¼ teaspoon lemongrass essential oil
¼ teaspoon juniper essential oil
½ teaspoon liquid yellow colour
½ teaspoon liquid green colour

## Moulds
Tennis ball cut in half

## Other ideas
**Other mould suggestions:**
*any round or half rounds*
**Other fragrance ideas:** *lemongrass, lavender, ginger, cypress essential oils*

Wake yourself up in the morning with a cappuccino bath bomb, but remember not to drink the bath water! Stimulating caffeine is used in many creams to help reduce the appearance of cellulite.

# *Cappuccino*

*See pages 24–26 for basic bath bomb recipe instructions*

## Ingredients

300g (11oz or 1 cup) granulated citric acid
600g (1lb 5oz or 2 cups) bicarbonate of soda (baking soda)
2 tablespoons of hot chocolate drinking powder
1 teaspoon instant coffee mixed with 1 teaspoon of water
½ to 1 teaspoon black coffee fragrance oil

## Moulds

Coffee mug-shaped chocolate-making mould

## Quantity

This recipe makes 4 large mug-shaped bombs

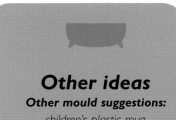

## *Other ideas*

**Other mould suggestions:**
*children's plastic mug*
**Other fragrance ideas:** *leave out the fragrance and let the coffee and chocolate powder scent the water*

Calling all chocoholics! Soak your body in pure, organic, fair trade chocolate, scented with sweet orange essential oil. Kids will love these chocolaty treats – add more chocolate for a truly decadent soak.

# Choccy Eggs and Chicks

See pages 24–26 for basic bath bomb recipe instructions

## Ingredients

300g (11oz or 1 cup) granulated citric acid
600g (1lb 5oz or 2 cups) bicarbonate of soda (baking soda)
1–2 tablespoons good-quality cocoa powder
1 teaspoon chocolate truffle fragrance oil
5g (approx 0.2oz or 1 teaspoon) melted cocoa butter
  (organic, unrefined if possible)

## Moulds

Egg-shaped bath bomb or soap-making mould
and chicken moulds

## Caution

Make sure these are labelled 'do not eat' and put out of reach of children.

## Quantity

This recipe will make approximately 6 regular-sized chocolate eggs and a small flock of 3 chickens

Having a bad day? Uplift your spirits with these pretty butterflies, symbols of the soul and a long life. Pop one into a warm bath, breathe in the exquisite aroma, lie back and let yourself float away.

# Up, Up and Away

*See pages 24–26 for basic bath bomb recipe instructions*

## Ingredients

300g (11oz or 1 cup) granulated citric acid
600g (1lb 5oz or 2 cups) bicarbonate of soda (baking soda)
¼ teaspoon neroli essential oil
¼ teaspoon palmarosa essential oil
¼ teaspoon rose geranium essential oil
¼ teaspoon black pepper essential oil
¼ teaspoon liquid red colour (or ultramarine pink powder)
   in half a batch of mixture

## Moulds

Butterfly moulds

## Additional instructions

Fragrance your recipe in the usual way and put half of the recipe into another bowl. Leave one half uncoloured and colour the other half pink and bind both batches with water in the usual way – you will need to move fairly quickly so that the mixture does not dry out. Fill one side of the mould with pink and the other with white. Alternatively you can colour some butterflies all white and others all pink. Note: If using ultramarine pink powder do not exceed the amount stated.

## Quantity

This recipe will make approximately 15 butterflies

You shall go to the ball... and if you have bathed in one of these sumptuous bath bombs with our aphrodisiac blend (see page 54), you are sure to attract the man or woman of your dreams.

# Having a Ball

*See pages 24–26 for basic bath bomb recipe instructions*

## Ingredients

300g (11oz or 1 cup) granulated citric acid
600g (1lb 5oz or 2 cups) bicarbonate of soda (baking soda)
1 teaspoon aphrodisiac essential oil blend (see page 54)
1 teaspoon cosmetic grade glitter
⅛ teaspoon cosmetic grade glitter hearts

## Moulds

Round bath bomb mould

## Quantity

This recipe will make approximately 4 round bath bombs using a regular-size mould

### Other ideas
**Other fragrance ideas:**
*clary sage, jasmine, patchouli, sandalwood and neroli essential oils*

If you are like me and can't eat just one fairy cake at a time, why not pop two or three of these moisturizing little fizzers into the bath and soak up the sweetness.

# Fairy Cakes

*See pages 24–26 for basic bath bomb recipe instructions*

## Ingredients

300g (11oz or 1 cup) granulated citric acid
600g (1lb 5oz or 2 cups) bicarbonate of soda (baking soda)
1 teaspoon raspberry fragrance oil
1 teaspoon raspberry seed oil
⅛ teaspoon liquid red colour
   (or ⅛ teaspoon ultramarine pink powder)
¼ teaspoon liquid yellow colour

## Caution

Make sure these are labelled 'do not eat' and put out of reach of children.

## Additional instructions

Fragrance your recipe in the usual way, add the oil and put half of the recipe into another bowl. Colour one half with the yellow, add your water, mix and mould. Then add your red or pink colour to the other half, mix and mould. Note: If using ultramarine pink powder, do not exceed the amount stated.

## Moulds

Fairy cake mould

## Quantity

This recipe will make approximately 16 fairy cakes

Pop one of these calming and warming pumpkin treats into the bath after a fun evening of trick-or-treating for your over-excited little 'monsters'.

# Pumpkin

*See pages 24–26 for basic bath bomb recipe instructions*

## Ingredients

300g (11oz or 1 cup) granulated citric acid
600g (1lb 5oz or 2 cups) bicarbonate of soda (baking soda)
1 teaspoon pumpkin seed oil
½ teaspoon liquid yellow colour
½ teaspoon liquid red colour
1 teaspoon sweet orange essential oil
1 teaspoon cinnamon powder (optional)

## Moulds

Pumpkin mould

## Quantity

This recipe will make approximately 6 pumpkin bombs

## *Other ideas*

**Other mould suggestions:**
*round balls/spheres*
**Other fragrance ideas:**
*pumpkin spice fragrance oil,
mandarin essential oil*

Using ingredients from around the world: orange blossom
for tranquillity; manuka, known to heal and prevent infection; grapefruit
for the immune system; and frankincense for inner peace and calm.

# Planet Earth

*See pages 24–26 for basic bath bomb recipe instructions*

### Ingredients

300g (11oz or 1 cup) granulated citric acid
600g (1lb 5oz or 2 cups) bicarbonate of soda (baking soda)
¼ teaspoon neroli essential oil,
¼ teaspoon manuka essential oil
¼ teaspoon grapefruit essential oil
¼ teaspoon frankincense essential oil
5g (approx 0.2oz or 1 teaspoon) melted shea butter
¼ teaspoon liquid green colour (or ¼ teaspoon
   chromium green oxide) in half of the mixture
¼ teaspoon blue liquid in the other half of the mixture

### Moulds

Round mould

### Additional instructions

Fragrance your recipe in the usual way, add the butter and put
half of the recipe into another bowl. Colour one half green
and the other half of the batch blue and add the water in the
usual way – you will need to move fairly quickly so that the
mixture does not dry out. Fill one side of a round with the
green mixture and the other with blue, press together and
unmould the sphere in the usual way. See pages 24–28.

### Quantity

This recipe makes 4 worlds

### Caution

If using chromium green oxide do not exceed the
stated amount.

The rose has been a symbol of love and beauty for centuries and used in skincare to promote cell renewal. This sensual and comforting blend of rose and jasmine will lift and soothe your spirits.

# Melt my Heart

*See pages 24–26 for basic bath bomb recipe instructions*

## Ingredients

300g (11oz or 1 cup) granulated citric acid
600g (1lb 5oz or 2 cups) bicarbonate of soda (baking soda)
1 teaspoon rose hip powder (optional)
10g (0.35oz or 2 teaspoons) melted shea butter
   or rose hip oil
½ teaspoon rose fragrance oil,
½ teaspoon jasmine fragrance oil
⅛ teaspoon Bach Flower Rescue Remedy
½ teaspoon liquid red colour
   (or ⅛ teaspoon ultramarine pink powder)
1 tablespoon rose petals

## Moulds

Heart-shaped mould

## Quantity

This recipe will make approximately 8 hearts

## Additional instructions

Sprinkle a few of the rose petals (you will need less than you think) in to the bottom of your bath bomb mould. Fill with mixture and turn out as usual

Melt my Heart

Are you feeling fruity? A mouth-wateringly juicy recipe with moisturizing mango butter to soften the skin — a unisex favourite for all ages.

# Mango Grove

*See pages 24–26 for basic bath bomb recipe instructions*

## Ingredients
300g (11oz or 1 cup) granulated citric acid
600g (1lb 5oz or 2 cups) bicarbonate of soda (baking soda)
1 tablespoon mango powder
1 teaspoon mango fragrance oil
5g (approx 0.2oz or 1 teaspoon) melted mango butter
½ teaspoon each of liquid red and green colour

## Additional instructions
Add all the ingredients except the colour and divide the mixture in two. Colour one half with ½ teaspoon liquid yellow colour and ½ teaspoon liquid red colour, and the other half with ½ teaspoon liquid green colour. Fill half of each mould with each colour, press together and gently turn out.

## Moulds
Large egg mould

## Quantity
This recipe will make approximately 4 mangoes

## Other ideas
**Other mould suggestions:**
*any size sphere or half round*

Calmly they went in two by two... just like your little ones into the bath. Mandarin essential oil is known to calm and soothe restless children, letting *you* have a peaceful night's sleep.

# Noah's Ark

*See pages 24–26 for basic bath bomb recipe instructions*

## Ingredients

300g (11oz or 1 cup) granulated citric acid
600g (1lb 5oz or 2 cups) bicarbonate of soda (baking soda)
½ to 1 teaspoon mandarin essential oil
½ teaspoon of liquid colour of your choice

## Additional instructions

Divide your mixture into two (or three colours if you are feeling particularly clever) and add approximately ¼ teaspoon of liquid colour to each half batch as required. Add water, mix and mould in the usual way.

## Moulds

Various animal moulds

## Quantity

This recipe will make approximately 10 animals

### Other ideas
**Other fragrance ideas:**
*sweet orange, lavender and chamomile essential oils*

Is there something fishy going on? Embed a plastic tropical fish in your bath bomb and surprise your family. When they pop it in the bath, listen for the laughter when a fish pops out and bobs around their bath tub.

# Goldfish Bowl

*See pages 24–26 for basic bath bomb recipe instructions*

## Ingredients

300g (11oz or 1 cup) granulated citric acid
600g (1lb 5oz or 2 cups) bicarbonate of soda (baking soda)
½ teaspoon liquid blue colour
1 teaspoon ocean, seaweed, or spa fragrance oil
Approximately 3 plastic fish

## Moulds

Large round mould

## Quantity

This recipe makes approximately 3 goldfish bowls

## Additional instructions

Half fill one side of a large round mould and gently press a small plastic fish into the mixture and then pile on more mixture as if making a regular round bath bomb. Fill the other side of the round and press together to make a large round. If you are not confident in turning out a large bath bomb, just remove the top half of the mould, let it harden for 30 minutes or so and then unmould.

## Caution

Make sure that you keep small parts away and out of reach of young children.

Goldfish Bowl

Hide some nasty plastic flies, spiders or bugs in your bath bombs and hear the screams when they pop out in the bath. You might not get any supper, but it may be worth it for the entertainment value.

# Don't Bug Me

*See pages 24–26 for basic bath bomb recipe instructions*

## Ingredients

300g (11oz or 1 cup) granulated citric acid
600g (1lb 5oz or 2 cups) bicarbonate of soda (baking soda)
1 teaspoon passionfruit fragrance oil
¼ teaspoon liquid blue colour
¼ teaspoon liquid green colour
Various plastic spiders, flies or bugs

## Moulds

Bee-shaped mould

## Quantity

This recipe will make approximately 6 bugs

## Caution

Make sure that you keep small parts away and out of reach of young children.

My favourite treat is a trip to a relaxing spa, but if like me you do not often get the chance, this recipe will help you create your own mini spa in your bathroom, relaxing your muscles and clearing your mind.

# Atlantic Spa

*See pages 24–26 for basic bath bomb recipe instructions*

## Ingredients

300g (11oz or 1 cup) granulated citric acid
600g (1lb 5oz or 2 cups) bicarbonate of soda (baking soda)
125g (4½ oz or ½ cup) Epsom salts
¼ teaspoon liquid blue colour
   (or non-smelling ultramarine light blue powder)
¼ teaspoon liquid green colour
   (or chromium green oxide powder)
1 teaspoon powdered kelp
½ teaspoon lavender essential oil
¼ teaspoon cypress essential oil
¼ teaspoon rosemary essential oil

## Moulds

Rectangular shape with rounded corners

## Quantity

This recipe will make approximately 10 fizzing spa tablets

Create a tea party of bath bombs by displaying these cute muffins in your bathroom together with the fairy cakes (page 98) and green tea (page 85) bath bombs.

# Blueberry Muffin

*See pages 24–26 for basic bath bomb recipe instructions*

## Ingredients
300g (11oz or 1 cup) granulated citric acid
600g (1lb 5oz or 2 cups) bicarbonate of soda (baking soda)
1 teaspoon blueberry muffin fragrance oil
2 tablespoons goat's milk powder
5 tablespoons (or a small handful) of blue malva flowers

## Additional instructions
Using the muffin mould in one hand and the half sphere in the other, scoop the mixture into both sides and press together as you would for a round mould. Gently remove both halves and place in an apple storage crate, round side down.

## Moulds
Muffin mould for the base, and a half sphere for the top

## Quantity
This recipe will make approximately 5 blueberry muffins

After a hard day digging on the allotment or in your kitchen garden, soak away your aches and pains with an effervescent, aromatic plant pot-shaped bath bomb.

# Purely Potty

*See pages 24–26 for basic bath bomb recipe instructions*

### Ingredients

300g (11oz or 1 cup) granulated citric acid
600g (1lb 5oz or 2 cups) bicarbonate of soda (baking soda)
¼ teaspoon lemongrass essential oil
¼ teaspoon tea tree essential oil
¼ teaspoon lavender essential oil
1 teaspoon comfrey powder
¼ teaspoon liquid green colour
   (or ⅛ teaspoon chromium green oxide powder)

### Moulds

Plastic flower pots from a garden centre

### Quantity

This recipe makes three large pots and 6 mini pots

## Other ideas
**Other mould suggestions:**
*yoghurt pots*
**Other fragrance ideas:**
*any herbaceous or citrus essential oils*

Make a herby ball with your favourite herbs and flowers. Pop each little bomblet in a muslin bag, toss into a warm bath, and the muslin bag will contain any herbs and flowers that may clog up your plug.

# Herb Garden

*See pages 24–26 for basic bath bomb recipe instructions*

### Ingredients

300g (11oz or 1 cup) granulated citric acid
600g (1lb 5oz or 2 cups) bicarbonate of soda (baking soda)
2 tablespoons dried chamomile flowers
2 tablespoons dried calendula (marigold) flowers
2 teaspoons dried nettle herb
2 teaspoons dried parsley herb
1 to 1½ teaspoons of our herb garden energy
    and concentration blend (see page 55)
Muslin or organza bags to hold the bombs

### Moulds

Small round bath bomb moulds

### Quantity

This recipe will make approximately 14 bomblets

*Note:* Because we have used small bath bomb moulds in this recipe you can increase the amount of essential oils used in this recipe to 1½ teaspoons of essential oil blend.

This anti-fungal foot blend is perfect for sporty types to freshen up.
Once you have soaked your feet, exfoliate with a foot brush and apply
a soothing moisturizing cream for the twinkliest toes around.

# Twinkle Toes

*See pages 24–26 for basic bath bomb recipe instructions*

## Ingredients
300g (11oz or 1 cup) granulated citric acid
600g (1lb 5oz or 2 cups) bicarbonate of soda (baking soda)
1 tablespoon chamomile powder
1 teaspoon anti-fungal aromatherapy foot blend (see page 54)

## Moulds
Any mould

## Quantity
This recipe will make approximately 10 fizzing tablets

Let your little angels say 'wishy washy, let's get sploshy', then sprinkle in the fizzy powder and make a wish. *Your* wish may then come true as they are sent off to slumberland for a whole night's sleep.

# A Washy Wish

*See pages 24–26 for basic bath bomb recipe instructions*

## Ingredients

300g (11oz or 1 cup) granulated citric acid
600g (1lb 5oz or 2 cups) bicarbonate of soda (baking soda)
½ to 1 teaspoon lavender essential oil
½ teaspoon cosmetic grade glitter
¼ teaspoon cosmetic grade glitter stars
¼ teaspoon liquid blue colour and ¼ teaspoon
   liquid red colour or ¼ teaspoon ultramarine violet
   or ½ teaspoon liquid purple colour

## Additional instructions

Measure out all of the ingredients and thoroughly mix in the bowl. Tip the ingredients into a plastic bag and leave overnight. If your mixture has hardened, seal the top of the plastic bag and lightly bash the contents with a rolling pin until they are a powder. If the weather is dry and without much humidity your mixture may remain as a powder and you will not need to crush it. Store the magical dust in a dry, plastic tub or bag.

## Quantity

This recipe will make 900g (2lb) of magical dust

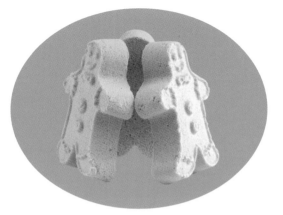

A spicy little number for those winter blues. Warm yourself by soaking with one of these cute little comforting gingerbread bath bombs, put on your fluffiest slippers and sit by the fire with a cup of hot cocoa.

# Winter Warmer

*See pages 24–26 for basic bath bomb recipe instructions*

## Ingredients

300g (11oz or 1 cup) granulated citric acid
600g (1lb 5oz or 2 cups) bicarbonate of soda (baking soda)
½ to 1 tablespoon ginger powder
¼ teaspoon liquid yellow colour
¼ teaspoon liquid red colour
1 teaspoon ginger spice, or similar, fragrance oil
   or ¼ teaspoon ginger essential oil, ¼ teaspoon black
   pepper essential oil, ½ teaspoon sweet orange essential oil

## Moulds

Gingerbread man mould

## Quantity

This recipe will make approximately 8 gingerbread bath bombs

## *Other ideas*

**Other mould suggestions:**
*rounds, yoghurt pots, any other moulds*
**Other fragrance ideas:**
*any spicy, warming, gingery scents*

A traditional winter drink full of soft sweet spice and warm wine to be enjoyed on a dark winter evening. If you want to feel a little spicy, submerge yourself in a tub filled with this warm exotic scent.

# Mulled Wine

*See pages 24–26 for basic bath bomb recipe instructions*

## Ingredients

300g (11oz or 1 cup) granulated citric acid
600g (1lb 5oz or 2 cups) bicarbonate of soda (baking soda)
1 teaspoon cinnamon powder (optional)
1 teaspoon nutmeg powder
½ teaspoon liquid red colour
⅛ teaspoon liquid green colour
½ teaspoon winter spice fragrance oil
¼ teaspoon strawberry fragrance oil
   (or sweet orange essential oil)
1 tablespoon red wine (optional)

## Moulds

Plastic wine glass

## Quantity

This recipe will make approximately 2–3 bombs

### Other ideas
**Other fragrance ideas:**
*nutmeg, clove, cinnamon, ginger, clementine or mandarin essential oils*

If you are a budding film star, uplift your spirits whilst treading the boards. It is a long journey to Hollywood, so why not pat yourself on the back and award yourself a glittering, aromatic gold star.

# Make me a Star

*See pages 24–26 for basic bath bomb recipe instructions*

## Ingredients

300g (11oz or 1 cup) granulated citric acid
600g (1lb 5oz or 2 cups) bicarbonate of soda (baking soda)
½ teaspoon lemongrass essential oil
½ teaspoon grapefruit essential oil
½ teaspoon liquid yellow colour
¼ teaspoon cosmetic grade gold glitter
⅛ teaspoon cosmetic grade glitter stars

## Moulds

Star-shaped soap-making mould and star-shaped ice cube moulds

## Quantity

This recipe will make approximately 10 regular-sized stars

Meet me under

If you want to give your friend or loved one a secret message, hide it in a bottle-shaped bath bomb and when the bath bomb erupts it will pop out and surprise the bather.

# Message in a Bottle

*See pages 24–26 for basic bath bomb recipe instructions*

## Ingredients

300g (11oz or 1 cup) granulated citric acid
600g (1lb 5oz or 2 cups) bicarbonate of soda (baking soda)
½ teaspoon liquid green colour
Folded message written on plastic with waterproof ink
1 teaspoon aloe and cucumber fragrance

## Moulds

Bottle-shaped chocolate-making mould

## Quantity

This recipe makes 5 half-bottles

## Additional instructions

Write your message on a piece of plastic or pvc shopping bag.
Fold it up and insert in the middle of your bomb.

Use your imagination and creativity to make different-shaped sea creatures only found in the depths of the mystical deep blue ocean and let them join you in the bath.

# Beneath the Sea

*See pages 24–26 for basic bath bomb recipe instructions*

## Ingredients

300g (11oz or 1 cup) granulated citric acid

600g (1lb 5oz or 2 cups) bicarbonate of soda (baking soda)

2 tablespoons sea salt or Dead Sea salt (ground in a pestle and mortar if necessary)

1 teaspoon oceanic-type fragrance oil

1 teaspoon liquid colour of your choice

## Additional instructions

Divide the mixture in two and colour one half with ¼–½ teaspoon of liquid blue colour and the other half with ¼–½ teaspoon liquid red colour. Use both colours in each mould to create a two-tone effect. See page 31.

## Moulds

Various mermaid, fish and shell moulds

### Other ideas
**Other fragrance ideas:**
*any oceanic fragrance or lavender*

With the scent of gardenia, bring Tahiti to your bathroom. Imagine mountain peaks reaching over dense rainforests of soft ferns with waterfalls cascading into cool streams surrounded by tropical flowers.

# South Pacific

*See pages 24–26 for basic bath bomb recipe instructions*

## Ingredients

300g (11oz or 1 cup) granulated citric acid
600g (1lb 5oz or 2 cups) bicarbonate of soda (baking soda)
1 teaspoon gardenia fragrance oil
5g (approx 0.2oz or 1 teaspoon) melted Monoi de Tahiti

## Moulds

Lotus flower

### Other ideas
**Other suggestions:**
*any floral mould or half sphere*

## Quantity

This recipe will make approximately 7 flowers

Bring back memories of that exotic holiday with this tropical piña colada cocktail bath bomb scented with coconut, rum and fruity pineapple.

# Piña Colada

*See pages 24–26 for basic bath bomb recipe instructions*

## Ingredients

300g (11oz or 1 cup) granulated citric acid
600g (1lb 5oz or 2 cups) bicarbonate of soda (baking soda)
⅛ teaspoon liquid red colour
⅛ teaspoon liquid yellow colour
1 teaspoon pina colada fragrance oil
1 teaspoon rum (optional)

## Moulds

Any plastic cup, or yoghurt pot

## Quantity

This recipe will make approximately 3–4 piña colada bombs

### Other ideas
**Other fragrance ideas:**
*blend pineapple and coconut fragrance oils together*

Relax, unwind and de-stress in a bath scented with intoxicating floral aromas. Absorb some of nature's theraputic power and let your worries soak away.

# Flower Power

*See pages 24–26 for basic bath bomb recipe instructions*

## Ingredients
300g (11oz or 1 cup) granulated citric acid
600g (1lb 5oz or 2 cups) bicarbonate of soda (baking soda)
¼ teaspoon rose geranium essential oil
¼ clary sage essential oil
¼ black pepper essential oil
¼ frankincense essential oil
¼ teaspoon Bach Flower Rescue Remedy
½ teaspoon liquid colour of your choice

## Moulds
Various flower moulds

## Additional instructions
Divide the mixture in two and colour one half with ¼ teaspoon liquid red colour and the other half with liquid purple colour or ¼ teaspoon of ultramarine lilac.

## Quantity
This recipe makes 9 flowers

# Recipe guide

| Recipe name | Fragrance/ essential oils | Additives | Colour | Mould |
|---|---|---|---|---|
| Milky Whey page 82 | Roman chamomile and lavender essential oils | Whey and goat's milk powder; Vitamin E | None | Star and moon moulds |
| Green Tea page 85 | Green tea fragrance oil | Green tea powder | Liquid green | Teapot-shaped (chocolate) mould |
| Snowtime page 86 | Snow fragrance oil | Glitter | None | Snowflake, snowball |
| Game, Set and Match page 88 | Lemongrass, grapefruit and juniper essential oils | Wheatgrass powder | Yellow and green liquid | Tennis ball cut in half |
| Cappuccino page 91 | Black coffee fragrance oil | Instant coffee | Chocolate drinking powder | Half round bath bomb mould or coffee cup (chocolate) mould |
| Choccy Eggs and Chicks page 93 | Chocolate truffle fragrance oil | Cocoa butter | Cocoa powder | Egg bath bomb mould and chicken soap moulds |
| Up, Up and Away page 94 | Neroli, palmarosa, rose geranium and black pepper essential oils | None | Liquid red | Butterfly soap moulds |
| Having a Ball page 97 | Aphrodisiac blend from perfume section, see page 54 | Glitter and glitter hearts | None | Medium round bath bomb mould |
| Fairy Cakes page 98 | Raspberry fragrance | Raspberry seed oil | Yellow and red liquid | Fairy cake bomb mould |
| Pumpkin page 101 | Sweet orange essential oil | Cinnamon powder and pumpkin oil | Yellow and red liquid | Pumpkin mould |
| Planet Earth page 102 | Neroli, manuka, grapefruit and frankincense essential oils | Shea butter | Blue and green liquid | Medium round bath bomb mould |
| Melt my Heart page 104 | Rose fragrance oil and jasmine fragrance oils | Bach Flower Rescue Remedy, rose petals, shea butter or rose hip oil | Liquid red | Heart moulds |
| Mango Grove page 107 | Mango fragrance oil | Mango powder and mango butter | Liquid yellow, red and green | Large egg bath bomb mould |
| Noah's Ark page 109 | Mandarin essential oil | None | Liquid colour of choice | Animals – dogs, fish, lion, frog |
| Goldfish Bowl page 110 | Ocean, seaweed or spa fragrance oil | Plastic goldfish | Liquid blue | Large round |

| Recipe name | Fragrance/ essential oils | Additives | Colour | Mould |
|---|---|---|---|---|
| Don't Bug Me page 113 | Passionfruit fragrance oil | Plastic spiders and flies | Liquid blue and green | Bee moulds |
| Atlantic Spa page 114 | Lavender, cypress, rosemary essential oil | Kelp (seaweed) powder; Epsom salts | Liquid blue and green | Bar mould |
| Blueberry Muffin page 117 | Blueberry muffin fragrance oil | Blue malva flowers and goat's milk powder | None | Muffin bomb mould and half sphere |
| Purely Potty page 118 | Lavender, lemongrass and tea tree essential oil | Comfrey powder | Liquid green | Plastic plant pots from garden centre |
| Herb Garden page 120 | Herb Garden Energy and Concentration blend from perfume section, see page 55 | Chamomile flowers, calendula flowers, dried nettle and dried parsley | None | Small round bath bomb mould |
| Twinkle Toes page 123 | Anti-fungal foot soak blend from perfume section, see page 54 | Chamomile powder | None | Any |
| A Washy Wish page 125 | Lavender essential oil | Glitter and glitter stars | Liquid blue and red | None |
| Winter Warmer page 126 | Ginger Spice fragrance oil | Ginger powder | Liquid yellow and red | Gingerbread man mould or round |
| Mulled Wine page 129 | Winter spice fragrance oil and strawberry fragrance oil | Cinnamon powder and nutmeg powder, red wine | Liquid red and green | Plastic wine glass |
| Make me a Star page 130 | Lemongrass and grapefruit essential oil | Gold glitter and glitter stars | Liquid yellow | Star soap moulds and star ice cube trays |
| Message in a Bottle page 133 | Aloe and cucumber fragrance oil | Message written in waterproof ink on piece of plastic bag | Liquid green | Bottle (chocolate) mould or plastic drinks bottle cut in half. |
| Beneath the Sea page 134 | Oceanic type fragrance oils | Sea salt or Dead Sea salt | Liquid colour of choice | Various mermaid, fish, seahorses and shell moulds |
| South Pacific page 136 | Gardenia fragrance oil | Monoi de Tahiti | None | Lotus flower mould (or other floral mould) |
| Piña Colada page 139 | Pina colada fragrance oil | Rum (optional) | Red and yellow liquid | Plastic cup or yoghurt pot |
| Flower Power page 141 | Clary Sage, black pepper, frankincense essential oils | Bach Flower Rescue Remedy | Liquid red, purple, blue or colour of choice | Various flower moulds |

*Recipe guide*

# Suppliers

Many pharmacies and health food shops will supply essential oils and herbs for use in cosmetics. Bicarbonate of soda (baking soda) can sometimes be obtained from the natural cleaning sections of shops and citric acid may also be obtained from companies that supply ingredients and equipment for home brewing.

The following are a list of mail order/internet-based companies; the addresses provided are their trading addresses which are warehouses and are not open to the public unless specified.

## UK

**Amphora Aromatics**
36 Cotham Hill
Cotham
Bristol
BS6 6LA
tel: 01179 047212
www.Amphora-aromatics.com
*Wide range of essential oils and aromatherapy supplies*

**Aromantic Ltd**
17 Tyler Street
Forres
Moray
IV36 1EL
tel: 01309 696900
www.aromantic.co.uk
*Wide range of ingredients*

**Bach Original Flower Remedies**
Head Office
Nelsons House
83 Parkside, Wimbledon
London, SW19 5LP
tel: 020 8780 4200
www.bachremedies.co.uk
*Bach flower remedies are also available from many pharmacies and health food shops*

**Bathbomb biz Ltd**
37 Worting Road
Basingstoke
Hampshire
RG21 8TZ
tel: 01256 474889
www.bathbombrecipe.co.uk
*Ingredients and moulds*

**Cakes Cookies & Crafts Shop**
Unit 8, Woodgate Park
White Lund Industrial Estate
Morecambe
Lancashire
LA3 3PS
tel: 01524 389684
www.cakescookiesandcraftsshop.co.uk
*Huge range of fun chocolate moulds*

**G. Baldwin & Co.**
171/173 Walworth Road
London
SE17 1RW
tel: 020 7703 5550
www.baldwins.co.uk
*Herb specialists established in 1844, vast range of herbs with a high street shop*

**Gracefruit**
146 Glasgow Road
Longcroft
Stirlingshire
FK4 1QL
tel: 01414 162906
www.gracefruit.com
*Unusual ingredients and fragrances*

**Just A Soap**
South East Lodge
Rede Road, Whepstead
Bury St Edmunds
IP29 4ST
tel: 01284 735043
www.justasoap.co.uk
*Ingredients and moulds*

**Sheabutter Cottage**
Unit 3
Sonning Farm
Charvil Lane
Sonning, Reading
RG4 6RH
tel: 01189 693830
www.sheabuttercottage.co.uk
*Fair trade oils, butters and other ingredients*

**Soap Basics**
23 Southbrook Road
Melksham
Wiltshire
SN12 8DS
tel: 01225 899286
e-mail: info@soapbasics.co.uk
www.soapbasics.co.uk
*Bath bomb ingredients, fragrances, additives, colour and moulds*

**The Soap Kitchen**
Units 2 D&E Hatchmoor Industrial Estate
Hatchmoor Road
Torrington
Devon
EX38 7HP
tel: 01805 622944
e-mail: info@thesoapkitchen.co.uk
www.thesoapkitchen.co.uk
*A wide range of ingredients, moulds, oils, butters, colour, herbs and fragrance*

**The Soapmakers Store**
Unit 13, Lawson Hunt Estate
Guildford Road, Broadbridge Heath
Horsham
West Sussex
RH12 3JR
tel: 0844 800 3386
www.soapmakers-store.com
*Ingredients and moulds*

**Soap School**
20 The Grove
Fartown, Huddersfield
West Yorkshire
HD2 1BL
tel: 01484 310014
e-mail: sarah.janes3@ntlworld.com
www.soapschool.com
*Large supply of moulds, including a bespoke service*

# US

**Bramble Berry Inc.**
2138 Humboldt Street
Bellingham
WA 98225
tel: 360/734-8278, Toll Free: 877-627-7883
www.brambleberry.com
*Very wide range of ingredients, fragrance, oils and moulds*

**Camden-Grey Essential Oils Inc.**
3579 NW 82 Ave
Doral, FL 33122
tel: orders 866-503-8615 enquiries 305-500-9630
e-mail: orderdesk@camdengrey.com
www.camdengrey.com
*Wide range of essential oils, absolutes and moulds*

**Costal Scents**
K-Plex LLC
935 3rd Avenue North
Naples
Florida 34102
tel: 239-214-0181
www.coastalscents.com
*Bath bomb and cosmetics supplies*

**Cranberry Lane**
50-2268 No 5 Rd.
Richmond, BC
V6X 2T1
tel: 1-800-833-4533 / 604-944-1488
www.cranberrylane.com
*Large supply of ingredients and moulds*

*Suppliers*

**Custom Chocolate Shop**
RR 2 Box 2378
Canadensis, PA 18325
tel: 570-595-2880
e-mail: kristin@customchocolateshop.com
www.customchocolateshop.com
*Large range of chocolate moulds, including personalized moulds*

**From Nature With Love**
Natural Sourcing, LLC
341 Christian Street
Oxford CT 06478
tel: 800-520-2060 or 203-267-6061
www.fromnaturewithlove.com
*Ingredients and moulds*

**Herbal Accents**
PO Box 937
Alpinie, CA 91903-0937
tel: 619-562-2650
e-mail: sales@herbalaccents.com
www.herbalaccents.com
*Ingredients and moulds*

**Kangaroo Blue**
12407 Rhea Drive, Units 102–103
Plainfield, IL 60585
tel: 815-609-9275
www.kangarooblue.com
*Moulds, some ingredients, essential oils and additives.*
*Can pick up pre-ordered goods from warehouse*

**Majestic Mountain Sage**
918 West 700 North Ste 104
Logan, Utah 84321
tel: 435-755-0863
www.thesage.com
*Botanicals, moulds, fragrance*

**Milky Way Molds**
PMB #473
4326 SE Woodstock
Portland, OR 97206
tel: 503-774-4157
e-mail: contact@milkywaymolds.com
www.milkywaymolds.com
*Designers and manufacturers of a huge range of unique, fun moulds*

**Snowdrift Farm Inc.**
2750 South 4th Avenue
Suites 107 & 108
Tucson
Arizona 85713
tel: 888-999-6950 / 520-882-7080
www.snowdriftfarm.com
*Ingredients and moulds*

**The Chemistry Store**
1133 Walter Price St
Cayce, SC 29033
tel: 800-224-1430
e-mail: sales@chemistrystore.com
or glitter@chemistrystore.com
www.chemistrystore.com
*Ingredients*

**The Essential Oil Company**
8225 SE 7th Ave
Portland
Oregon 97202
tel: 800-729-5912 / 503-872-8735 / 503-872-8772
www.essentialoil.com
*Essential oils and moulds*

**The Scent Works**
PO Box 828
Durham
North Carolina
27702-0828
tel: 1-973-598-9600
e-mail: Sales@TheScentworks.com
http://store.scent-works.com
*Large range of fragrance and essential oils, herbs, oils, butters and botanicals*

# Australia and New Zealand

**Aussie Soap Supplies**
PO Box 165
PALMYRA WA 6957
tel: (08) 9339 1885
e-mail: david@aussiesoapsupplies.com.au
www.aussiesoapsupplies.com.au
*Wide range of ingredients and moulds. Visits to workshop by appointment*

**Australian Bush Flower Essences**
Bush Biotherapies Pty Ltd
45 Booralie Road,
Terrey Hills, NSW, 2084
tel: (02) 9450 1388
e-mail: info@ausflowers.com.au
www.ausflowers.com.au

**Big Tree Supplies**
4/30 Denman Street
Alderley QLD 4051
tel: (07) 3352 4395
e-mail: info@big-tree.com.au
www.big-tree.com.au
*Moulds and fragrance oils*

**Essential Oils and Soap**
7 Beaton St
Exeter
Tasmania 7275
tel: (03) 6394 3737
e-mail: info@oilsandsoap.com.au
www.oilsandsoap.com.au
*All ingredients for bath bomb making*

**Heirloom Body Care**
78 Barnes Road
Llandilo NSW 2747
tel: (02) 4777 4457
e-mail: heirloom@heirloombodycare.com.au
www.heirloombodycare.com.au
*Bath bomb ingredients and moulds. Visitors by appointment*

**Manuka Oil.com**
Bio-Extracts Ltd
PO Box 5
187 Mill Road,
Bombay, South Auckland
New Zealand
tel: (09) 236 0917
e-mail: email@ManukaOil.com
www.manukaoil.com
*Manuka oil*

**Nature Shop**
10 Japonica Road
Epping
NSW 2121,
tel: (02) 9869 1807
www.natureshop.com.au
*Essential oils, botanicals and other oils*

*Suppliers*

# Further reading

Many of the herbal recipes in some of the older books should be used as reference only, as modern herbal medicine has advanced hugely since the books were written and some of the information may now be inaccurate.

Ashenburg, Katherine, *The Dirt On Clean: The Unsanitized History* (North Point Press, 2007) ISBN: 978-0-37453-137-9
An interesting and light-hearted history of bathing from early Greeks and Romans to the present.

Briggs, Margaret, *Bicarbonate of Soda: A Very Versatile Natural Substance* (Black and White, 2007) ISBN: 978-1-84502-163-4
The science and varied uses, including natural cleaning recipes, personal use and cooking with bicarbonate of soda.

Culpeper, Nicholas, *Culpeper's Complete Herbal: A book of natural remedies for ancient ills* (Wordsworth Editions Ltd, 1995) ISBN: 0-572-02794-X 90100
Seventeenth-century herbal remedies by the famous London apothecary, physician and astrologer, Nicholas Culpeper (1616–1654).

Grieve, Mrs M (F.R.H.S), *A Modern Herbal* (Merchant Book Company Ltd, 1973) ISBN: 1904779 01 8
First Published in 1931 by Jonathan Cape Ltd. Revised edition 1973. A well-known, in-depth herbal reference book from the early twentieth century with detailed information on each herb, including medicinal uses, folklore and origins.

McVicar, Jekka, *New Book of Herbs* (Dorling Kindersley, 2004) ISBN: 978-1-40530-579-2
How to grow and harvest your herbs, with culinary and cosmetic uses and recipes with a look at 100 top herbs in detail.

Rimmel, Eugene, *The Book of Perfumes* Elibron Classics Series (Adamant Media Corporation, 2005) ISBN: 14021-7820-4
This edition is an unabridged facsimile of the edition published in 1865 by Chapman & Hall, London. A truly fascinating and easy-to-read nineteenth-century book on the history of perfume.

Smith, Bruce and Yamamoto, Yoshiko *The Japanese Bath* (Gibbs M. Smith, 2001) ISBN: 978-1-58685-027-2
Everything you ever wanted to know about Japanese bathing – you will definitely want to have one built in your house after reading this book (I am saving up).

Various, *Herbs for Use and for Delight: An Anthology from the Herbarist* (The Herb Society of America) ISBN: 0-486-23104-6
A selection of articles from the Herb Society of America's publication *The Herbarist* including a history of perfume, dyeing with herbs and detailed articles on 25 specific herbs.

*The New Guide to Remedies* (Parragon, 2003) ISBN: 978-140542-160-7
Homeopathy, essential oils, crystals and home remedies.

# Safety

The ingredients used in making bath bombs are safe for external use. However, if you do get any citric acid, bicarbonate of soda or essential oils in your eyes or in an open wound or cut, it will sting so you should place your eye or affected area under water and irrigate for ten minutes. If symptoms persist, seek medical advice.

The remedies and therapeutic information in this book are based on general historical and reported information and should never be treated as a substitute for conventional medical advice. Care should be taken when using essential oils, herbs, botanicals and other additives with medication, mental illness, or other conditions such as high blood pressure, epilepsy, pregnancy, lactation and for children under the age of 16 or the elderly.

Thought should also be given if you are giving a bath bomb to a friend or family member who might not know what it contains. Always list your ingredients so that you do not give a product as a gift with an ingredient that may cause an adverse reaction to someone's condition of which you are perhaps unaware, for instance early pregnancy or if they are taking medication.

It is most important that all of your ingredients, blends and bath bombs are clearly labelled and stored away from children and pets.

# Selling

The information and recipes in this book are to enable you to produce your own bath bombs for home use only. Bath products come under the umbrella of the pharmaceutical and drug industries and there are strict regulations in most countries if you wish to sell your products.

For instance, in Europe, all bath products must be safety assessed and then certificated by a cosmetic chemist or toxicologist and registered with Trading Standards involving stringent labelling legislation, weights and measures, manufacturers details, batch numbers, record keeping, health and safety and insurances and may not make any medical claims. However, regulations vary around the world, and can also change, so if you are wanting to make products for sale you should fully investigate all of the appropriate trading legislation of your country and any other countries that you are wishing to sell to.

*Safety and selling*

# Glossary

**Ablution**

The act of washing or cleansing the body either in a daily cleanliness routine or as part of a religious ritual for the purpose of purification.

**Antioxidant**

An antioxidant is a molecule that can slow or prevent the oxidation of other molecules thereby counteracting the negative and damaging effects of oxygen. Antioxidants such as vitamin A, C and E, can neutralize the effects of free radicals which can contribute to ageing and health problems.

**Aroma chemicals**

Synthetically produced elements of a perfume or fragrance developed in the late nineteenth century to replicate the more expensive and hard to find essential oils and other ingredients, such as animal scents or rose.

**Aromatherapy**

A form of complementary therapy that applies essential oils to help ease health complaints and conditions.

**Astringent**

From the Latin 'astringere', meaning 'to bind fast'.  An astringent is a substance which can shrink, contract or draw together body tissues. They are used as a 'toner' to firm and tone the skin, constricting the pores and protecting the skin. An astringent can soothe the skin, shrinking mucus membranes thereby reducing swelling and relieving skin irritation.

**Ayurvedic**

Considered by many to be the oldest form of alternative medicine, Ayurvedic medicine is a form of traditional Hindu healthcare practised in the Indian subcontinent for more than 5,000 years and through diet, exercise, lifestyle and cleansing is used to balance the body, the senses, mind and soul.

**Base note**

Base notes are the group of fragrance ingredients that combine to provide the 'theme' of a perfume and are generally woody or resinous materials that will be the last scents to be detected, lingering the longest and 'fixing' the whole perfume blend.

**Botanicals**

The dried parts of plants, such as the leaves, flowers, peel, berries, seeds, roots and bark that are used for their therapeutic properties.

**Diuretic**

A substance that stimulates the production and elimination of urine, helping to purge the body of excess fluid.

**Emollient**

A substance or ingredient that softens the skin, preventing it from becoming dry, and slowing the evaporation of water.

**Enfleurage**

A process which captures the fragrant compounds of flowers and plants by infusing the aromatic blossoms in deodorized solid fats.

### Essential oils

Natural volatile liquids containing the concentrated aromatic compounds, or 'essences' of plants, leaves, fruit, seeds, roots, wood, resin, gum, grasses and flowers which are used in the food, cosmetic and pharmaceutical industries.

### Humectant

A hygroscopic substance which attracts water from the air and holds it within the skin, thus preventing the skin from losing moisture and drying out.

### Middle note

Middle notes are a group of fragrance ingredients that blend together to provide the heart and body of a perfume and become apparent to the nose after the top notes begin to disappear. They are usually warm, soft and mellow, rounding off the perfume to give it complexity.

### Mucilage

A soft, moist, viscous secretion or glutinous sap produced by plants believed to aid in their water storage and seed germination. Some of the richest sources are cacti, aloes and flax seeds. Mucilage is also found in mallow, comfrey and nettle. Mucilage is a natural emollient and is known to soothe dry, rough skin.

### Olfaction

This is the word used to describe our sense of smell. Volatile chemicals, or odours, travel up the nasal passages to the olfactory system and sensory cells which trigger messages to the brain which then tell us if the odour is dangerous or pleasurable, etc.

### Pheromones

A chemical substance produced by an animal or insect which triggers a natural physiological or behavioural response in another of the same species.

### Phototoxic

A chemical compound with enhanced toxicity when exposed to ultra-violet light (sunlight, tanning lights) which may cause skin reactions such as burning, irritation, or pigment changes. Most of the citrus essential oils, bergamot in particular, are phototoxic.

### Pomade

Probably originating from the French word 'pomade' meaning ointment, pomade is fat that has been infused with the scent of flowers by the process of 'enfleurage'. It is a greasy substance that was widely used in the first half of the twentieth century to style and condition the hair.

### Top note

The top notes, or head notes, are the group of fragrance ingredients that are the first odours that hit you on sampling a perfume. Assertive, bright and initially strong, they create the first impression of a fragrance. These fresh, sharp top notes are powerful and intense to begin with, but are the first scents to disappear in a perfume.

### Volatile

Essential oils are usually described as 'volatile' oils, which are plant-derived odorous compounds, or the aromatic scents of plants, that evaporate or vaporize readily in nature.

## About the author

Elaine Stavert formed The Littlecote Soap Co. after a life-changing move from her television career in London to a farm in the beautiful Buckinghamshire countryside. Surrounded by hedgerows and meadows and with a keen interest in herbalism and aromatherapy, Elaine was soon developing a range of natural toiletries and bath products that were both kind to the skin and quintessentially English. Elaine's passion for her products is evident in the pure and natural ingredients that are used in imaginative ways to produce traditional recipes with contemporary twists.

The Littlecote Soap Co.
Littlecote Farm
Littlecote
Nr Dunton
Buckingham
MK18 3LN
**www.littlecotesoap.co.uk**

## Acknowledgements

Robert, my mother and Pearl
For love, encouragement and support.

I would also like to thank the wonderful team at The Littlecote Soap Co., my business partner Pearl Olney, Nikki Jellis, Rebecca Gulliver, Carole Capel, Jess Bliss, for their hard work and dedication, and in particular Caroline Heron for the use of her hands and nose in the book and for proofreading each section. My thanks also to all those at Littlecote Farm; Alison Vintner in the office, Sean Jackman and Mr Nab for their sense of humour and for introducing me to a whole new array of natural aromas. Sue Lister from Lister Communications, Sarah Janes from Soap School, Richard Phillips from The Soap Kitchen and Lisa Wright from The Gallery for their shining pearls of wisdom and professional advice. And finally to Benjamin Hedges from J. Hedges and Sons for reminding us of traditional values and without whom the company would not exist.

My grateful thanks also to the talented team at GMC Publications, to Jonathan Bailey and Gerrie Purcell for inviting me to write this book, to Gilda Pacitti and Jo Patterson for their creative eye for detail and design, Hedda Roennevig for picture research and much more and editor Virginia Brehaut for her skill, professionalism and patience.

## Photographic acknowledgements

Main project photography by Laurel Guilfoyle

Step-by-step photography by Elaine Stavert and also on pages 18, 32, 37, 39 (right), 41 (right), 42, 43, 44, 45 (left), 59 (middle top and bottom), 64 (left), 67 right column, bottom 3, 68 far left, 75 (left), 76 (right), 77 (left), 78, 79 (left).

All other photography by Anthony Bailey, except as below:

GMC Publications would like to thank the following for pictures used in this book: Toast, www.toast.co.uk: page 12, Mary Evans Picture Library: page 13, The Roman Baths: page 14, Cagaloglu Hamam, Turkey: page 15, Japan National Tourist Organization: page 16, Finnish Sauna Society: page 17, Michael Bevens: page 40 (left), www.morguefile.com: page 67, left column and top right, Virginia Brehaut: 58, 59 (right)

GMC Publications would also like to thank the following people who kindly loaned props for photography:

Steamer Trading Ltd, Lewes, East Sussex
Gill Parris, Lucy Hermann, Kate Collyns, Tracey Hallett, Louise Compagnone, Gilda Pacitti, Gerrie Purcell, Rebecca Mothersole, Virginia Brehaut, Elaine Stavert and Laurel Guilfoyle.

# Index

Names of recipes are given in italics.

Index

Contact us for a complete catalogue, or visit our website:
GMC Publications Ltd, 166 High Street, Lewes, East Sussex BN7 1XU, United Kingdom
Tel: 01273 488005  Fax: 01273 402866
**www.gmcbooks.com**